A WRITER'
TO THE IN

Other Allison & Busby Writers' Guides

A WRITER'S GUIDE TO THE INTERNET

Trevor Lockwood and Karen Scott

a&b

First published in Great Britain in 1999 by
Allison & Busby Ltd
114 New Cavendish Street
London W1M 7FD
http://www.allisonandbusby.ltd.uk

A catalogue record for this book is available from
the British Library.

ISBN 0 7490 0444 4

Typeset by DAG Publications Ltd, London.
Printed and bound in Great Britain by
Biddles Ltd, Guildford.

CONTENTS

1

INTRODUCTION

This book is addressed to writers. It is about the internet and its message is simple: *there is a revolution going on and as a writer you need to be part of it.* We want to open your eyes to the profound changes that are taking place in the use of the written word and to help you to grasp the opportunities open to you. We will also remove the jargon and mystique that surround the internet.

Every writer should have access to the internet. It is a valuable source of information – from the strong and authoritative right across the spectrum to the wild and wacky – and it will help you to contact agents and publishers, to find out what is going on, to link up with other writers and to reach markets. And it is a place to publish. The internet is hungry for content; for original material, for well-written work, for careful research and for fresh perspectives. There is gold out there in the web. (There is also a lot of base metal.) We offer a prospector's guide.

We look at the internet through the eyes of a writer. We will clear away the confusion and help you to distinguish between the valuable, the not-so-valuable and the worthless. We will not talk down to you but we will keep things simple. We will make it possible for you to develop working partnerships on the web and teach you how to be efficient in your research. We will help you to set up a website and show you how to promote it so that you have a steady flow of visitors.

You will need a computer with a modem and a telephone line. Access is usually gained through an **internet service provider (ISP)**. There are hundreds of ISPs to choose from and many of them now offer free services. They all maintain a permanent link to the internet and most of them provide an email service, collecting and storing the emails sent to your email address.

If you are buying, buy the best computer you can afford. The internet is designed to be used with relatively simple equipment but higher operating speeds and larger storage capacity will make things easier for you. You will be linked to the internet through a network or a modem. Most home computers are modem based. Make sure you have a good modem. The modem converts computer files into small 'packets' of information and squirts them down the telephone line. At the other end of the line another modem converts the information back into a readable computer file.

But you can explore the internet without owning a computer. Most library services now have internet terminals which can be hired by the hour. And there are also 'cybercafés' where you will find the same facilities with plenty of people willing to give you free advice. You may want to explore the internet before buying your own machine.

A brief history of the internet

Most of us find the internet difficult to grasp at first. That doesn't matter. It is really no more than a network of computers linked together and able to share information and communicate with each other. It is like a telephone system, except that the internet can send and receive text, pictures, video and audio as well as speech. The essence of the internet is its ability to transfer and store large amounts of data.

In 1969 US military leaders decided that they needed to be able to communicate quickly with their troops during times of conflict. Under the threat of nuclear war, it was very important that everyone received clear orders and could remain in contact with their command structure even when a control centre had been destroyed. Computers were seen as the best way of preserving such links, allowing a rapid transfer of information quickly and accurately to many different locations at the same time. Radio, telephone and telegraph were more vulnerable, more open to misinterpretation, difficult to link together. Postal communication was too slow.

Then universities became interested in this new network; it was clear that ideas and information could now be communicated rapidly and efficiently. The new system remained in military and academic hands for a time but the news of its potential was spreading. New methods of use and access began to develop.

We must be grateful to the groups of pimply youngsters who huddled around their electronic boxes, often working in bedrooms or garages. This youthful fervour gave us huge companies like Microsoft and super-nerds such as Bill Gates, now one of the richest and most powerful men in the world. Obsessive tinkering and experimenting gave us the internet, an information revolution perhaps comparable to the development of the printing press in 15th century Europe.

The new systems enabled computers to transfer files and to share information but it was still a technicians' paradise, using arcane techniques and a strange language that was difficult to learn. This denied access to most people and it seemed as if the new computer networks would remain in the hands of specialists. (Even today, the computer specialists in some large companies hold more power than they should.)

The World Wide Web

Then the personal computer, the PC, was born. The first PCs appeared in the 1970s but in 1981 IBM developed the hardware and software for the independent, 'stand-alone' machines which would dominate the market. The PC, and its elegant rival the Apple Macintosh (1984), have developed at a furious rate, but they remain recognisable descendants of those first machines. The next step was that these machines should be linked together so that they could communicate directly with each other without having to print out or to transfer from disks or tapes. Companies began to link machines together for such functions as accounts, administration and production controls. This exchange of information brought greater speed and accuracy as well as major economies. And each employee could now gain direct access to needed information without delay. A managing director could have a more accurate picture of current activities within the company. At the same time, military and academic users were extending their use of computer networks.

And so the internet grew. By the late 1980s the term was used for any external network of computers for any purpose. Systems with strange names such as FTP (File Transfer Protocol), GOPHER (self-explanatory) and WAIS (Wide Area Information Servers) were developed to control the transfer of information. A turning point came in 1989 when the British scientist Tim Berners-Lee developed the **World Wide Web** at CERN (the European Particle Physics Laboratory, near Geneva). The WWW was designed for the high energy physics community but it spread rapidly and became the major component of the internet. Berners-Lee is now the managing director of the World Wide Web Consortium, an organisation that controls and ratifies the web systems.

The WWW keeps to the principle of universal readership. Once information has been published on the internet it must be accessible from any type of computer, by any person, in any country. This access must be through a computer program which is easy to use and freely available. The concept is simple but the realisation of it is highly complex. Fortunately the user does not need to know any of the elaborate protocols, transfers and technology that support the system. Television was like magic at first, and even today very few of us could explain how pictures arrive on our screens. Now we have to adjust to the fact that we can read a page from a computer in Australia and then casually flick over to a linked page from a computer in the US, or Japan, or Guatemala, while we sip a cup of coffee in front of our own computer in Chipping Camden. We all feel some nervous tension when we connect to the World Wide Web for the first time. But don't worry, it will pass. You may feel that you will be shamed by a lack of expertise. But users of the WWW are a tolerant bunch. They know how you feel and most of them haven't been using the net for long themselves. If you have problems, someone, somewhere, will be glad to help.

So there it is. The internet lies before you; waiting for you to find your own pathways through it; to discover your own favourite places to browse and make contact with like-minded people; to use it as a clinical tool for research or merely as a place to wander (marvelling at the strange excesses and obsessions on some of the websites); to find all the valuable contact addresses in your particular field. It will also provide you with a quick and cheap way of reaching friends and colleagues all over the world.

The rest of this chapter will give you some useful definitions.

Website

A **website** is a collection of pages, linked together but having one **domain name**.

The website, and all its pages, has a unique address, known as a **URL (Unique Reference Locator)**. No two are the same. The URL is in fact a long number but you will contact it by its domain name. URL addresses look complicated at first but they follow a similar pattern. Once you understand this you can break it down into its constituent parts. Let us take the example of our own site: http://www.author.co.uk. The **http** stands for **Hypertext Transfer Protocol** and is separated from the rest of the address by :// (a colon and two forward slashes); **www** (as you may have guessed) stands for the **World Wide Web**. Then follows the unique part of the address: **author.co.uk.** The domain name is **author**. This name is licensed and cannot be used by anyone else. (A domain licence, protecting the name, usually lasts two years and is renewable. Domain names can be purchased from suppliers, such as **www.netnames.com**.) The **co.uk** denotes a commercial organisation, located in the United Kingdom. The international version is **.com**, widely used by US companies.

Other suffixes include **.net**, **.ltd**, **.org**, **.gov**, and many more. Most countries now have their own unique two-letter identifying code.

To reach a website the URL for that site is entered in the top line of your browser. When you press the return key the computer will find the site and display its opening page (usually called the **homepage**) on your screen. Most browsers (the two major ones at the moment are Internet Explorer and Netscape) do not require you to enter **http://**. You can usually drop the **www** as well. In the example above you simply type **author.co.uk** and press the return key. You can also reach a website by clicking on a **link** from another website or by using a **search engine**. (These are explained in more detail below.) Once the website is on your screen it can be **bookmarked**. This places the URL in the Bookmark or Favourites folder of your browser so that you can reach it quickly in future.

Hypertext links

The concept of **links** was crucial to the World Wide Web. As you are reading one page of a website you are offered direct links to others, reached by clicking on the link itself. These links can serve many purposes. Let us suppose that you were reading an article about the PC. One link may take you to another website where there is more detail about monitors, another may offer you a biography of Tim Berners-Lee, a third may take you to 'the history of the PC' and a fourth may be a list of published books on the subject. You are offered choices of this kind all the time. And not all of them are text. Some of the links may take you to graphics, video, film or audio files. A good website will also have links to its own later pages.

It is not always necessary to enter a website through the homepage. Most sites have several sections, with the files for each section contained within a 'folder'. These sections can be accessed through the folder's name. To go back to our example: http://www.author.co.uk/karen will take you directly to the Karen Scott section of our website. This folder will have its own homepage, usually called **index.htm** or **default.htm**. The browser will display that page first.

There is another level below the folder, that of the individual 'file'. Each web page is made up of a **.htm** (or **.html**) file to which are attached all the other elements of the page. If we were to add a particular file extension to our own URL, for example http://www.author.co.uk/circles.htm, it would lead directly to a page listing Writers' Circles in the UK. The **circles.htm** is a specific page reference. The suffix **.htm** or **.html** is similar to **.doc** or **.txt** on other computer files but it indicates that this particular file is written in **Hypertext Mark Up Language**, the language of the World Wide Web. HTML language enables one computer to display what it receives from another computer in a common format. It will look more or less the same on any computer. It can also handle a mass of different displays so that they are understood by different computers. Until the arrival of HTML it was difficult for computers to display information in the same way.

Negotiations about allowable formats on the web are still going on. Most of them are irrelevant to most of us. But for the specialists, data formats are being designed to handle, for example, DNA codes, the spectra of stars, the design of bridges and even Classical Greek. People working in these fields have software enabling them to view, manipulate, analyse and modify such specific data.

Search engines

The internet is not a controlled library. There is no one checking and improving the content; it is simply a hotch-potch of HTML files that have been made accessible by millions of individuals, companies, organisations and governments. Each has its own reason for displaying information. Pages from the White House, the National Gallery or the Society of Ancient Druids are on the internet for different purposes. There is no unifying logic. The internet is very young and very incomplete. It can be a confusing environment. To help you to find your way, search engines have been developed. There are at least 900 already. Most of them are commercial operations, on the internet to make money in one way or another. They acquire information in different ways. Some, such as the widely used **Yahoo.co.uk.**, rely on submissions inviting their team of validators to examine a particular website. If the site meets Yahoos's criteria, it will be included in their index. Other search engines send out webcrawlers, fiendish little programs that visit websites and index every word on every page.

These engines are becoming more sophisticated, allowing a more precise selection of sites. The user of a search engine is asked to enter words that will define their area of interest. The search normally uses a Boolean logic sequence so that several words can be linked together to make an efficient search. (George Boole, 1815–64, was an English mathamatician and logician who developed his 'logic' as a kind of algebra for the manipulation of sets.) The search engine will look for any references that contain the words you have specified. Within seconds the search engine will produce a list, beginning with the top 10–20 sites containing those words. It will also tell you the total number of pages that contain your search word. If you were to enter, say 'horse' and 'racing', the response would run into millions. But if you want to know whether a particular jockey is riding at Ascot today you can be much more specific. You would enter **Delaney** (the jockey's name), **Ascot, racing** and the date. The answers you receive will be usable but there will still be links to a huge variety of irrelevant sites. Links to national and sporting online papers, to tipsters, to the jockey's own personal website and maybe a spattering of strange references, including a history of marathon running written by a Percy Delaney who lived in Ascot some years ago.

New generations of search engines are already offering new possibilities. One index, www.dogpile.com, will search other search engines and present you with a coherent list if the reference is very obscure. Other new developments are search engines that determine which sites are the most popular in your chosen field, and others that can distinguish which sites are for or against a particular argument.

Portal sites

Portal sites such as **live.excite.com** or **crayon.net** provide an opening page to a web browser that can be tailored to individual needs. Portals may become more important. If the portal site has a steady stream of users, it will attract advertisers and in addition to this the site owner has the chance to create a page of useful links to meet his or her own needs. Such developments are in their early stages but they will improve the quality of searches.

Email

When you are linked to the internet you can have your own email address. An email address is made up of two parts, such as trevor@author.co.uk. The **trevor** part refers to the individual owner of the email address. It is always separated from the domain name by @. So the same domain can also receive mail addressed to karen@author.co.uk. Email is a vital function of the internet and is its most widely used element. While you are connected to the internet you are paying the telephone company at the local call rate. So it is best to compose your emails 'offline' where they can be placed in a folder and transmitted when you connect up to your service provider. (You could prepare hundreds of messages this way and then transmit them all over the world for the price of one local call.) One individual email can be sent to a particular address while simultaneously sending copies to several other addresses. Emails offer the speed of the telephone with the permanence of a letter, leaving you a file copy.

And now to the business of writing

Most of the information in this opening chapter has been relevant to all internet users. We now move on to information which is specific to writers.

2

MAKING CONTACT WITH OTHER WRITERS

Where to begin

Now that you have some idea of how to set yourself up on the internet, the concepts behind using it and the use of search engines, it should quickly become obvious that the writer need never feel lonely again. Gone are the days of looking at a blank page or screen convinced that you are alone in the world, terrified that writer's block may set in at any moment. Go and make yourself a cup of coffee and search the web for other literary minded people; discover that the internet really is a writer's haven.

The other thing to remember is that the internet and the web, as their names indicate, really are web-like structures that are all interconnected in some way. Searching for a chat room may lead you to an interesting newsgroup, which may then lead you to a writer's website, or a site that offers an online writing course or a critiquing service.

Your main problem from then on will probably be overload. So many new ideas, concepts and pieces of information to grasp, and for a short while it will be hard to translate them into any kind of order, let alone take them all in. So for the time being it is best to bookmark anything that particularly interests you and go through the list at your leisure. Netscape runs a Bookmark system – where the titles or URLs of websites can be stored. When you are visiting a website that you want to return to at a later date – open the Bookmark menu and select 'add Bookmark'. The site will be added to a list underneath the main menu. It's that simple.

Internet Explorer, Microsoft's answer to Netscape, provides a history of the pages you have visited and if the files are held in the cache you can even view them offline. So with a record of where you have been it is easy to find pages again. This facility, however, only stores pages for a limited time. If you want to keep a permanent link to the page you must add it to your list of 'Favourites'. It is also cheaper to download pieces of information to read later, instead of looking at them while the clock is ticking away.

Websites for writers about writers

There are too many websites for writers on the internet for them to be listed in any detail. But there are sites that stand out from the crowd: reference and research sites, some of the societies and ezines, critiquing services and support or advice sites. The best way to find your way around is to use one of the big directories such as **Yahoo (UK & Ireland)** at http://www.yahoo.co.uk; this has links to over a million pages. Type what you are looking for in the box provided and it will conduct a search for you; each main heading will lead to a second level and so on. **Infoseek** has an extra search precision facility, which enables you to search websites, newsgroups, news or companies. Chose a category and type a writing-related topic or word into the box and hit 'search'.

Personal choice will attract you to one site instead of another. Use your own instinct when roaming around the web. There is no regulatory body that oversees the internet so you will have to rely on your own judgement. The shelf-life of some sites may be short, either because they are not updated regularly or because they have been removed or have developed a technical hitch. In the last cases you will be given an 'error' message when you type in the URL.

Search engines are also available to help you to hunt for like-minded people and relevant places. These include **Infoseek**, **AltaVista**, **Lycos**, and **Excite**, amongst others. The art is to narrow the search down to pinpoint exactly what you are looking for as quickly and easily as possible. Most of these search engines have help facilities that will point you in the right direction. A particularly reliable search engine is **WebCrawler** (http://webcrawler.com); this service secures its information from a 'spider', which travels the web looking for new pages. Successful use of the WebCrawler means refining your search by using 'and', 'or' and 'not' to link the search words. Also try using www.dogpile.com, a search directory of search directories.

Reference sites

These sites are self-explanatory and allow you to access a whole range of media, from encyclopaedias to dictionaries and a host of other reference material which you may find useful when doing research. There are some excellent sites to be found. Listed below are a few to help you to get started, but this is not a definitive list, there are many more!

Internet Public Library

A first for the internet; run by librarians so they know what they're doing. Offers a broad base of services similar to a mainstream library.
http://www.ipl.org/

Reference Shelf

This site provides information on films, television and radio. It also offers thesaurus and dictionary facilities.
http://astro.temple.edu/~pryluck/index.html

The Writer's Internet Resource Guide

This site is a good source of information – especially if you want everything under one roof.
http://novalearn.com/wirg/

The B & R Samizdat Express

Offers chat facilities, discusses internet trends and has a search engine. It offers many other internet resources for writers, a readers' room, links to sites that publish domain electronic texts, electronic books for sales and an author homepage.
http://www.samizdat.com/

If you are in Europe; for a faster response, connect to their mirror site in the United Kingdom –
http://www.uk.samizdat.com

Support and advice sites

The World Wide Web is linked together by many, many strands and any attempt to pigeonhole or categorise it is very difficult. The writing-related websites that are part of this huge conglomeration of information range from manuscript preparation to details of markets currently available on the internet and any number of topics in between.

Most of the websites to be found on the internet are US or Canadian based, but happily sites from around the world – including the UK – are added to the list every day. We list a few general sites, with no particular slant towards genre, that are based in the UK. They may offer links to the US and other markets, and vice versa. Most UK sites have 'co.uk' in the URL, but sometimes it is difficult to tell where the site originates until you look at it.

Writers Inc
Writers Inc have been involved in electronic publishing for ten years.
http://www.writers-inc.ndirect.co.uk/

Working Title Writers
Working Title Writers are a group of poets and artists in Cardiff. They are 'dedicated to promoting poetry'. They want to make sure that poetry regains its status as a first-class, mainstream means of communication.
http://www.workingtitle.demon.co.uk/

Online Writers Club
Even provides musical accompaniment!
http://angelfire.com/mi/cocoz/

Visit the OLAA, sister club to the OLWC, or Online Writers Club. OLAA stands for Online Artists Association.
http://members.xoom.com/asphian/olaa.htm

Pure Fiction
A good site about UK markets for writers.
http://www.purefiction.co.uk

The Society of Authors
An invaluable site for writers in the UK. This website give details of the Society, but also includes many topics related to writing, publishing, copyright, electronic rights, and multimedia.
http://www.writers.org.uk/society/index.html

Writers Guild of Great Britain
They request that you join, but offer advice and will act on your behalf should you require help with publishing contracts, etc.
http://www.wggb.demon.co.uk/

By going to any of these sites you will find links to other sites. Remember to bookmark a site you want to return to; it is all too easy to wander from one site to another and then find it impossible to backtrack.

Genre sites

You can also search for information within your own particular genre. Listed below are sites that may be of interest to you; but there are many more to be found. These sites offer valuable information that may not be found so easily anywhere else.

Internet Crimewriting Network
The ultimate crime-writing resource. Bulletin boards, question-and-answer pages, new crime jargon, interviews with experts and more.
http://www.hollywoodnetwork.com/Crime/

Screenwriters' & Playwrights' Homepage
Resources include tips from professionals, discussion groups and practical information about these writing genres.
http://www.teleport.com/~cdeemer/scrwriter.html

Write Page
The WritePage is an online newsletter with over 300 pages of author and book information for readers and how-to information for writers of genre fiction.
http://www.writepage.com/

The Literary Times
Romance, romance, and more romance.
http://www.tlt.com

Travel Writers
This is a resource dedicated to the needs of travel writers, photographers and members of the travel industry. Provides information about markets and tips on improving writing. It really is a guide to the best resources for travel writers on the net.
http://www.travelwriters.com/

Fantasy Writers Discussion Group
A good UK source for fantasy writers. Last updated 23/03/1998 but still worth a look.
http://www.geocities.com/Area51/Labyrinth/5096/

Children's Writing Resource Centre
A good all round source of information for children's writers. Has a chat facility and many links.
http://www.write4kids.com/

Society of Children's Book Writers & Illustrators
For people who write, illustrate, or are interested in children's litera-

ture. This is a no-nonsense site, with very clear objectives.
http://www.scbwi.org/

Story Exchange
Contains short stories and gives writers a chance to submit their own work for publication on the site.
http://storyexchange.paconline.net/

Impetus Theatre
Market for new plays and writers.
http://www.btinternet.com/~impetus.theatre/

The Poetry Kit
Who's who in poetry.
http://poetribe.derwentside.org.uk/

Independent Radio and Drama Productions
Britain's leading independent producer of radio drama. This is a non-profit making company. This site is worth taking a look at even if you don't write drama or for the radio; you may find it opens up markets that you never knew existed.
http://www.irdp.co.uk/

Critiquing services

There are many critiquing and editorial appraisal sites for writers on the internet. They provide a valuable service and they also offer access to online courses and other information, but they vary a great deal in hype and charges. If you want to have your work looked at by a professional you will probably have to rely on your own instincts in your choice. It pays to be realistic though; they promise the earth but they cannot produce the goods if the writing is poor. Writers have to be honest with themselves in the first place. And take the advice you are given. Don't fool yourself into thinking that they don't know what they are talking about – they do – many of them are published writers themselves. Writers in general seem to have reservations about paying for an appraisal service; it is important to bear in mind that editorial and literary advice of this nature is not something you pick up by surfing the web. Appraising written work is a specialised job and requires a professional fee.

Martin Noble Editorial

The flashing graphics disguise a very professional service. Also requests, politely, that you sign a petition against land-mines.
http://www.martinob.demon.co.uk/

Advice and Criticism Service

Authors' consultants; detailed and constructive assessment of type-scripts. Provides advice regarding publiction.
http://www.hilaryjohnson.demon.co.uk

First Look

Allows you to fill out an electronic inquiry form – if they're interested in your material in the first instance they will let you know.
http://firstlookagency.com/default2.htm

Professional Literary Services

Has a section on improving your internet image.
http://home.earthlink.net/~wordking/

And finally . . . 'a little light relief'

At times even writers need to take time off.

Annual Interactive Fiction Competitions Website

Take a look at this for a mind-expanding look at the possibilities that the internet has opened up.
http://www.afn.org/~afn55673/contest/

The Bulwer-Lytton Fiction Contest Home Page

Where 'www' means 'wretched writers welcome'.
http://www.bulwer-lytton.com/

Hinde Sight

This site is devoted to science fiction, movies and an eclectic mix of subjects. Take a look at the Duelling Dialogue section and get those literary taste buds salivating.
http://www.ozcraft.com/scifidu/

Chat rooms

Chat rooms, as the title suggests, are places where relative strangers can meet and talk online. It really is like talking on the telephone but instead of speaking you type your comments onto the screen for someone else to read and respond to. In chat, you have a special window on your computer where the conversation appears and you can type what you want to say into an individual box. When you click 'Send' your message will appear in the conversation box. You can join in conversations by entering a 'room', post comments on a bulletin board, or even create your own chat room.

The quality of conversations to be had can vary dramatically and tends to be better when the topic is clearly defined. Conversations cut across each other and even when there is only one other person involved there can be delays in getting a response. Some are open slather, others invitation only. All the big directories offer chat room facilities. It is best to investigate a variety of chat rooms and see what is on offer; each one varies in format and really it is up to personal choice which system may suit. Try the chat facilities offered by **Yahoo** http://chat.yahoo.com. Or **Infoseek's** 'webchat', which requires no plug-ins or downloads to access.

A cautionary note

People in chat groups can be quite undisciplined and even nasty. Tread carefully to begin with; introduce yourself politely and follow the basic rules. Be wary of agreeing to meet anyone you have met in a chat room without thinking of your own personal safety. Meet in a public place to begin with. Basically the same rules apply as with personal ads. Don't give your password to anyone, even if they say they work for your service provider. Bear in mind that most people on chat groups lie about themselves! The recommendation is that you start by taking a look at the writing-related chat room sites listed below.

trAce Online Writing Community

One of the best sites for online discussions about many issues to do with writing. They offer weekly online live discussion about writing issues. They also offer two different meeting times to cater for time zones. For more information you can contact them by email: trace@ntu.ac.uk.
http://trace.ntu.ac.uk

The Write up Café

This site is linked to the Tyneside Creative Writer Group. UK based. Puts writers' work on the site. They meet in person once a month, look out for dates.

http://www.jprice.demon.co.uk/

It is impossible to list all the sites that have chat room facilities available to writers or to judge their quality; a useful tip to note is that many websites for writers offer online discussion facilities alongside whatever else they may do. The best advice is to find the ones that interest you – listen to what other people are saying – go to sites recommended by ezines, or other sites or chat rooms and take a look. You may also find that your ISP has chat facilities that you can access from their homepage. These are a bit safer as your ISP may provide supervision.

Newsgroups and mailing lists

Newsgroups are used in much the same way as mailing lists and as there are over 20,000 Usenet and other newsgroups available on the internet they are forces to be reckoned with. Usenet, aka 'network news', is a world-wide distributed bulletin board system. Internet users around the world submit Usenet messages to 'newsgroup' and within a day these messages are delivered to every internet host that wants them. Usenet is a public playing field; everyone else can read everything you say anywhere in the world. So beware of giving too much information away. You may not be able to gain access to all of them since the news server at your service provider usually selects them. If there is a particular newsgroup you wish to join, a request to your ISP will probably bring results. These newsgroups are dedicated to any subject you care to mention and cover a wide range of interests.

As a subscriber to a newsgroup you can read articles by other people, post your own and respond to articles. Newsgroups and mailing lists perform pretty much the same task, although a mailing list sends an individual copy of each message to a subscriber. Newsgroup articles are transferred in bulk between the sites that act as news servers, and you can access these as required and download if you want to. The advantage they have over mailing lists is that you go to them, they are not automatically sent out to you. It is pro-active and if your mood dictates your search requirements then newsgroups may be for you.

Collabra, the news software in Netscape Communicator, allows for subscribed group lists to be held in the message centre and the search is made simpler by a 'Subscribe to Newsgroups' panel. With Internet Explorer the News is handled by the software used for Mail, typically Outlook Express. You may have to configure your system in the first instance to get them up and running. Click on the 'Newsgroups' button on the main window, then click on 'All' at the bottom and type a word into the box at the top of the page. When you see a group that interests you, select it and click 'Go To'. You will then return to the main Outlook screen with the group activated. Perseverance is the order of the day with many things on the internet, and you need patience! You may find it simpler to access newsgroups and chat rooms straight from a search engine or simply access the sites themselves and bookmark them. Listed below are a few to get you started.

Deja News
This really is a forum for discussion groups. Covering any topic you care to mention. Just put the word 'writer' in the search facility and you won't surface for days.
http://www.dejanews.com/

The Complete Reference to Usenet Newsgroups
A good guide to what is out there as far as newsgroups are concerned. This is not a news server. Remember your ability to access newsgroups will depend mainly on your internet provider.
http://tile.net/news/

Usenet Information Centre Launch Pad
A website that will help you access the newsgroups.
http://metalab.unc.edu/usenet-i/

Newsgroups are organised into about 20 major divisions, subdivided by topic and subdivided again and again. But they fall into a number of general categories, and that is probably the best place to start. The names of the newsgroups describe their focal point, so finding **alt** at the beginning of a newsgroup title would indicate that it was an alternative newsgroup set up because its topics are not covered by the general index or divisions. The first part of a newsgroup name is called a hierarchy because they are structured like hierarchies, starting from the top and working their way down to include all the subjects under the main grouping.
biz – groups to do with business, market related issues.

comp – deals with many aspects of computing, including hardware and applications. This is a huge newsgroup and has over 60 first level divisions, which then go on to split themselves up into many categories.

info – small group with very mixed aspirations, discussing topics ranging from hot issues in the States to the National Science Foundation whose hardware forms the backbone of the internet in the US.

talk – politics, philosophy and religion.

misc – health, education, jobs, etc.

news – a good supply of tips can be had here for new users.

Making sense of it all

The internet is an independent and autonomous environment, bringing together people with similar interests from across the world so that they can talk, do business or just hang out twenty-four hours a day. For the writer it is a wonderful technology. However, it will probably take some time before you begin to get a feel for the internet, understanding its idiosyncrasies and feeling at ease with all the possibilities that it offers, but once you do you will wonder what you did before you had access to it.

Another cautionary note! Remember that the internet has no disciplinary body (although it has several regulatory bodies, including an anti-spamming and an anti-pornography system) and is really an unorganised mass of material. Anybody can have a website or a homepage and it is worth bearing this in mind when you are searching through the internet. Be careful about giving credit card details unless a secure payment device is available. Don't be too hasty. Do research, ask other people that you come into contact with if they have heard anything of the critiquing site you are interested in making use of. Bad news travels fast. It is best to go to a reputable site, such as http://www.author.co.uk and start from there; at least then you know that to the best of the website author's ability only genuine links to other genuine people are included. Many newsletters and writing websites post warnings about scams or illegal spamming.

There can be a problem with copyright on the internet and you must be aware that your ideas are open to theft. But most genuine writers are too busy thinking about their own work to bother with other peoples'. Scaremongering can be just as damaging to the generally good work that the internet does as scams are. However, most people in the writing business on the internet are genuine, up front and not looking to make a quick or illegal buck. The main thing is to be sensible; if something doesn't sound right, it probably isn't. It is also useful to bear in mind that the same principles apply in the writing world on the internet as they do in mainstream publishing.

A final note: although the technology of the internet is so far advanced that many people seem incapable of grasping its intricacies, it actually has its basis in text; *to use the internet, people have to communicate in writing.*

3

EMAIL, MAILING LISTS, EZINES AND NETWORKING

Email

Email is the most important element of the internet. The World Wide Web may look attractive with its multimedia possibilities but it remains a fairly static display. It is email that glues the internet together, allowing rapid exchanges to take place between individuals and groups. It provides a system of communication that offers the spontaneity of speech while adding the restraint and consideration of the written word. It is unlike any other form of communication. An email mysteriously arrives in the mail box and can be read when the recipient chooses, either onscreen or printed. A click with the mouse opens up a screen upon which a reply can be typed. Another click sends that reply back to the sender's mail box where it too will wait patiently to be read. And you can use the attachment facility (usually indicated by a paper clip) to 'attach' one or several files to your email.

Email is brilliant! It allows quick yet considered responses, messages that can be sent to one person at a time, or a million. Messages can be forwarded, annotated, combined and stored away for future use in a filing cabinet that doesn't lose all the important bits down behind the drawer. It is so easy it can become overwhelming. So many messages pile into the mail box demanding attention that the business of life can be impeded.

More people in the UK chat to work colleagues and friends using email than in any other nation in Europe. North America has realised the potential offered by the internet, but Europe is catching up quickly. In the UK online connections increased rapidly once it was possible to obtain a free email account. If the cost of local and internet telephone calls were to be included in the standard rental agreement the true potential of the internet could begin to be realised. There is a strong lobby promoting this.

A permanent eddress
Internet service providers allow access to the internet and provide you with an email address: yourname@service.co.uk. An email address (or eddress) will quickly assume the same importance as your home

telephone number or postal address. It is a vital link that the rest of the world – literally – can use to reach you. It may be the only point of contact, as many people will never know your address or telephone number. Lose it or change it and your world could disappear. Sites such as **bigfoot.com** offer a permanent email address (eddress). This is useful, as yourname@bigfoot.com does not depend upon being linked to any particular server. The email address to which your bigfoot email points can be changed, allowing switches from server to server yet always retaining a permanent eddress. **Emails.net** takes this further by allowing the user to choose between thousands of domain names to create a personal email address.

Email is cheaper and quicker than the postal services (snail mail) and can offer the same level of security. The sender can ensure that the email sent has been received, and can encrypt the message so that only the named email addressee can open and read the message. It is a great way of keeping in touch with Aunty Ethel now that she has moved to Worthing and it can do much more. It can be sent in ASCII text format, which can be read by any computer email program, or in HTML, which allows all the slick presentation gimmicks found on web pages.

Email to fax and voice

A useful free site is at **tpc.int.** that allows email to send documents to conventional fax machines. Microsoft 95 users may be unaware that they have NetMeeting installed. This allows online speech between two linked users across the internet. That means that America can speak to China or Australia to England for the cost of a local telephone call. It also provides a Whiteboard that both sides can share to draw diagrams and much more. Explore NetMeeting, it may be useful.

Spam

Email has its own version of junk mail, often called spam. Unsolicited emails may suddenly appear in the mail box. These can carry dangerous computer viruses and it must be emphasised that attachments from unknown sources should *never* be opened. Some people call junk mail 'direct mail'. Unsolicited material appearing in mail boxes can be interesting. The direct mail industry relies upon the knowledge that 2 in every 100 people will respond to unsolicited mail. Imagine the delight when it was discovered that bulk email programs could send the same message to millions of mail boxes at the same time, all for the cost of a local telephone call. There has been considerable reaction against spamming and few respectable businesses now engage in the practice. It may allow thousands of people to be informed but it will make few friends and should be avoided. Most email programs allow spam messages to be monitored and ISPs will respond when told that spam emails are being sent from their services. There are several organisations fighting spam. The **spam.abuse.net** allows webmasters to include a graphic link to display the message 'Boycott Internet Spam'.

Targeted email

Spam can be annoying, and can even clog up the entire internet, slowing down access for everyone. It is similar to a more productive method in which the same message can be sent to a large number of people. Such emails can be unsolicited, as targeted emails or as press releases, or they may be mailing lists that can only be received on subscription.

Targeted emails can be very successful, and every writer should retain the eddress of everyone who sends them an email. Such contacts are unlikely to complain if they subsequently receive an electronic 'mail-shot' from you. Be sure that all its recipients will be able to read it if HTML is used, or provide an ordinary text alternative. Email messages allow links to websites if the full URL http://www.yoursite.co.uk is used or an email link can be created by adding mailto:trevor@author.co.uk. This allows the reader to click on the address and move straight from the email to the new location.

The targeted email need be no more than a link to a page on a website. It need say no more than 'Look at my new poems at http://www.yoursite.co.uk/poems/'. Such brief messages are unlikely to offend and leave the recipient free to choose whether to visit the website or not.

As a website develops – with new material and old material placed in archives but still available – a regular targeted bulk email can entice earlier email contacts to visit the site again. Emails can be highly focused and cost-efficient ways of keeping in contact with the growing community of interests attached to an active website.

Press releases

These targeted emails can also be used to send a press release to any number of media sources. Providing some care is exercised in selecting the list, journalists and literary editors should not object to receiving such an email. Information is grist to their mill after all, but make it easy for them. Providing an opening statement that immediately reveals the subject matter, together with links to web pages to obtain more detail, is all that is needed.

The press release need not be confined to conventional media sources. As the web is trawled for information any useful contacts should be carefully bookmarked. If possible also obtain a suitable email address and file it away in a separate 'useful contacts' folder. Periodically send these contacts an email to keep them updated. It is often better to send these emails individually, creating a new email for each contact. The process can be speeded up if the bulk of the message is prepared first and then 'cut and pasted' into each message, leaving just the personal parts of the message to be added. Personalised messages, sent one at a time, are always more effective. Although the internet offers contact with millions of people all over the world it has a unique attribute: each message addresses only one person. In that respect it is different from any other form of advertising. Use that facility wherever possible. The most useful contacts will be those with whom you form a close personal bond, even though you may never meet or even know in which country they live.

Mailing lists and newsgroups

The ability to send bulk emails makes mailing lists, newsgroups and ezines (electronic magazines) possible. When you complete a subscription form, make sure that you do not reveal too much personal information, because there is no control once it is released. When you are accepted as a subscriber to a mailing list messages will start arriving in your mail box. These lists can be moderated, with the list owner deciding which messages should be included. They can be sent as individual messages, or condensed together into a digest of all the messages sent during a set time period, perhaps once a week. The subscribers can respond to all subscribers, or just to one person. They allow useful discussion to take place between subscribers and can be valuable resources.

Mailing lists use email to distribute messages and are very similar to newsgroups. These are a group of messages sent to news servers, computers run by companies or individuals, which can often host thousands of newsgroups. There are newsgroups for practically every subject and anyone can post messages. They are rarely moderated and the ISP decides which newsgroups can be accessed. They can be very useful ways of acquiring and disseminating information but they sometimes lack the cosiness of email mailing lists, which tend to have a smaller membership, allowing you to feel part of an online community.

Ezines

An ezine is an electronic publication and can also be called an electronic magazine, zine, webzine, fanzine or rag. It is solely or partially available online and is publicly accessible, usually on subscription. Electronic material available on the internet is usually free of charge. Sometimes an ezine is an online version of a print periodical or it may be a regularly published electronic magazine, journal, newsletter, newspaper or report that exists solely online. Some ezines are electronic publications created in a traditional print magazine format, others are simply regularly distributed email newsletters.

They can be produced in a many electronic forms and presentation can get very complicated if the ezine is to be designed to be readable everywhere. Standards are being accepted slowly. Normal ASCII text, which any computer can understand, is the simplest, and can be the most satisfying for the writer, as it relies upon writing skills.

The ezine can also be created in HTML, within an email program. This allows colour, different fonts, graphics and other facilities to be used. Visually it is more exciting but it requires some graphic design skills, and may not always display as intended on other computers. In both cases links can be imbedded into the text to allow readers to click to websites, download files, fill in forms or send emails.

Adobe Acrobat is popular among ezine publishers. The viewing software that online readers need to view the ezine is free, easy to obtain and it runs on almost all computers. An Acrobat Exchange kit must be purchased in order to create an ezine. Acrobat files are often referred to as **.pdf** files. Such ezines can be delivered using **ftp (file transfer protocol)** which offers fast and easy download.

Editing and producing an ezine is a useful way to keep abreast of developments and to be in touch with people who are interested in a particular subject. Keep early editions simple, as it can take as much time to produce an ezine as it does to produce a conventional print magazine, and it requires skills that are complex to use and time-consuming to acquire.

Use newsgroups, email and your website to advertise the ezine's existence. Free mailing list providers such as **topica.com** and **listbot.com** will provide all the facilities initially required. As the ezine develops you may wish to move towards a more sophisticated system, such as that available at **lyris.com**. Submit details of the ezine to search engines and to sites that specialise in listing online periodicals, such as **dominis.com.**

Networking: discussion groups, chat and IRC

There are a number of places where messages can be placed on public display. Mailing lists and newsgroups have already been mentioned but **Bulletin** and **Message boards** are slightly different. Usually associated with a website, they offer the same facilities as a newsgroup, in that responses to an original message will gradually form a **thread** all attached to each other. It is very easy to follow the course of the discussion by slipping from one message to the next. These discussion groups can be created to cover any subject, and they can be moderated and restricted to subscribers that have been accepted into the group.

Chat forums can also be attached to a website and are often used to allow an individual author to be contacted online, perhaps to discuss a latest book or to cover a specific question, or just to chat with friends. These call for good manners; several hundred people could all be logged into a discussion at the same time. Clearly they cannot all 'talk' (transmit their typed contributions) at the same time, but in spite of the difficulties they usually work very well. A moderator usually has the ability to remove unwanted guests or those that are hogging too much space.

Internet Relay Chat allows instant online communication and is provided from several sources. Once registered with **AOL Instant Messenger** you can communicate directly with friends using the system. As messages are typed and sent they appear within a split screen on both computers, enabling instant two-way communication. The program allows groups to communicate and for private areas to be created. Annoying or offensive message senders can be quickly excluded.

Some networks are less personal but they still allow groups of website owners to join together to display information about their own sites on sites owned by other members of the Ring. These **Rings** are essentially banner adverts that display on web pages. Every time the page is visited another site on the Ring is displayed in the banner. In that way each member of the Ring gains exposure on other sites. The quality of these associations depends upon the moderator of the facility. Badly managed Rings can result in some bizarre sites being displayed on your web pages.

Guests, polls and questions

Guest pages, online polls and questionnaires are also important parts of networking. Each will provide the site owner with valuable email addresses that can be used later to update those visitors who have shown a clear interest in the activities of the site.

The guest page provides a simple form for the site visitor to complete, to include their email address and to log a brief comment about the site. The site owner retains the provided email address. The comment is posted on to the Guest Comments Page, unless it is vitriolic or obscene. Site owners should post most of the bad along with the good, as honesty will encourage more constructive opinions and make interesting reading. They should take note of the responses, and make any changes to the site that seem necessary. Then send an email telling the guest of the improvements made as a result of their suggestions.

Online polls can ask visitors to vote on any subject. They add interest and variety to a website. A collection of poetry could be displayed and each visitor asked to choose a favourite. The winning poem could become a star feature at the end of the week or month.

Questionnaires follow the same format as those asked by shivering women standing outside supermarkets. They can provide site owners with information. Their design requires some skill. If there are too many questions – especially those that seem either too personal or irrelevant and questions that allow ambiguous answers – your responses will be disappointingly few or unusable. If the site owner says when the results will be available, this will encourage visitors to return to the site.

For the beginner the internet may seem a very difficult place. Full of confusing links, many of which are of little relevance. Remember that the web is still in its infancy, but that it is improving. A few hours invested in moving around the web should reveal some useful places that can be used as starting points from which to move on to other sites. In time you will build up a network of useful contacts and these will become vital to your business as a writer. There will be sites that specialise in offering jobs to writers, others where you can become engrossed in discussing a particular genre, still more where you know you will meet friends. The virtual community is the perfect place for writers. There is no longer any need to stand beside the garden fence chatting to a boring neighbour about scab on his tomatoes. The internet allows you to click away the mundane and concentrate, amongst friends, upon all that you regard as important. Why not join together with some of these new friends to create a mailing list or ezine or share any of the other facilities provided by the internet?

The web has developed its own dialect, and this may develop into a new international language. You need critical thinking when using the internet; there are few controls on the validity of its content. Be sceptical; be aware that all is not as it may seem. Do not release too much personal information until you are confident that it will not be abused.

4

ONLINE LITERARY MAGAZINES

The concept of the ezine

The concept of online publications or ezines is very similar to print-based subscription writing magazines; the format is similar and they provide the same basic facilities. They can also disappear off the shelf or the screen just as quickly. But the similarity ends there. Ezines arrive in your mail box with comforting regularity. When you have finished reading them you can delete them, or else you can copy them to another folder for future reference. Using links provided within the ezine you can leap to any number of websites or other ezines and take a look at something that catches your interest. You can visit other writers' homepages and check out their work, or you can submit your own manuscript to an ezine that is looking for the kind of article you may have just written. You can send emails to subscribe to other ezines or email an author who is undertaking a similar type of research to yours and compare notes. And all this before lunch; the possibilities are endless. This is the strength of electronic magazines and mainstream publications cannot hope to compete with them.

Ezines generally originate from a website and come to you from that site in the form of an email. So when you check your mail you will find, along with your personal and business email, any ezines you have subscribed to. If you click on them, they will open in the same way as any other email. Obviously it would not be cost effective to read them online, so it is best to file them in a separate folder and read them when you have time.

Finding ezines

Although here we are mainly concerned with ezines about writers and writing, ezines are not limited to the subject of writing and publishing. They cover a multitude of subjects and those ezines specifically about writers and writing also embrace a vast range of subjects from editorial matters to the finer points of poetry writing. The joy of ezines is that they often deal with themes that would never have seen the light of day without the internet.

Many ezines provide basic information and a forum for writers to discuss their opinions, others allow writers to showcase their fiction, poetry or other work. Ezines encompass a wide variety of styles and genres, and subscription is a matter of personal preference. The wonderful thing about ezines in general is that they provide a constant source of information and they also furnish new markets for the writer to exploit. They keep writers in touch with each other and they allow a free flow of information unlikely to be seen in the conventional printed magazine world. As every writer will discover there are very few print-based writing magazines that put writers in touch with each other as efficiently as the internet does.

You may find that your ezine subscriptions will fall into several categories.

- General interest
- Writing information
- Markets
- Genre

Once you have decided your area of interest and the markets you would like to target, you can begin your search. There are websites that have directories of ezines and this is as good a place to start as any. Many US-based ezines for writers are about making money – not a bad thing of course – but if you are interested in the more esoteric nature of writing then you may have to refine your search a little.

Ezine AdSource
Although this is primarily a site to advertise your ezine it does have a list over 400 ezines. If you decide to create an ezine of your own this is where to advertise it.
http://www.ezineadsource.com/d6pages/div6main.htm

Nerd World Media
Ezines – arts and entertainment resources from Nerd World Media.
http://www.nerdworld.com/nw1507oo60.html

Directory of Ezines
A comprehensive list of advertiser-friendly ezines.
http://www.lifestylespub.com/cgi-bin/ezines.cgi?10783

EzinePromote
Includes directories and other ways to promote your ezine.
http://www.onelist.com/viewarchive.cgi?listname=EzinePromote

Alternatively, you can begin your search by using **Yahoo** or **Infoseek** or one of the other search engines. Simply typing 'ezine' into the search box will probably provide enough material to keep anyone happy for weeks. Also, and this where the internet really comes into its own, you can search for lists of ezines using the Usenet website. You will be looking for 'alt.ezines'. It is also worth bearing in mind that many writing-related websites also produce their own ezines and provide links to other ezines. So, if you have a favourite website check out its ezine possibilities.

The Complete Reference to Usenet Newsgroups
Simply type 'alt.ezine' into the search box, although you may have to refine your search to find writing-related ezines.
http://tile.net/news/

Subscribing to ezines

Subscribing to ezines is almost as easy as finding them. Most ezines provide you with this information at the top of the ezine or on the last page. Each ezine may have its own requirements but generally it amounts to sending them an email with the word 'subscribe' in the subject box of your email, as described below.

Inscriptions
The weekly ezine for professional writers.
http://come.to/InscriptionsMirror
http://members.aol.com/maidenfate/Inscriptions.html
To subscribe, send an email to Inscriptions-subscribe@onelist.com.
To unsubscribe, send an email to Inscriptions-unsubscribe@onelist.com.

This means that you will be added to their list and will receive an electronic copy of the ezine in your mail box whenever they issue them, weekly, monthly or whatever. If you get fed up with any ezine, you can unsubscribe as above or simply replace 'subscribe' with 'unsubscribe' in the subject box of your email.

Ezines for writers who want to make money!

Ezines provide an entertaining and informative read for many writers but they may also provide a good supply of work. So, for instance, while you may want to read the review of Terry Pratchett's new book, you should also check out the section that ezines often refer to as 'markets' or 'fiction market' and 'non-fiction market'. This is where magazines online or otherwise ask interested writers to submit work. They also give detailed guidelines on the submission of manuscript/copy and the kind of work that is likely to be accepted. A fee scale is also listed, usually an amount per word. When you are looking for markets do not restrict yourself to online magazines, as many print-based magazines use the internet to advertise for writers too.

Write Markets Report
Magazine of new and updated markets and articles on selling the written word and making money through writing. Welcomes new writers. Free subscription. Sample free by email (forwriters@hotmail.com).
Also *National Writer's Monthly* is available from this site.
http://www.writersmarkets.com

The Quality Books Newsletter
This site is not specifically to do with writing but does provide masses of information about the internet, legal matters and a host of other topics. Subscribe by sending an email to majordomo@mLists.net with 'subscribe qualitybooks' in the body of the message.
http://www.qualitybooks.com

Pif
As one reviewer put it, Pif 'is fast becoming the litmus test for new authors on the net'. A show-case for quality poetry and short fiction by new and emerging writers, looking for original, well-thought-out pieces. They accept all kinds of writing on an unsolicited basis.
http://www.pifmagazine.com

Reader's Digest
They are always on the lookout for contemporary stories. Pay on acceptance. Buys exclusive world periodical rights, electronic rights, among others. Editorial lead-time is three months. Submit seasonal material six months in advance. Non-fiction: book excerpts, essays, exposé, general interest, historical/nostalgic,

humour, inspirational, interview/profile, opinion, personal experience. Buys 100 mss/year. Query with published clips. Does not read or return unsolicited mss. Length: 2,500–4,000 words. Original article rates generally begin at $5,000. For more information, contact Reader's Digest, Reader's Digest Rd, Pleasantville, N.Y. 10570-7000. Phone (212) 450-7000 or email readersdigest@notes.compuserve.com.
http://www.readersdigest.com

Reader's Digest is most definitely not to be sneered at, especially when you consider how much they pay for an article!

The MoJo Wire

This is a site for the politically motivated writer. It is a US-based ezine and has nothing to do with the subject of writing. Story ideas should engage issues that are in the news. As they say, if you use your imagination, they might just pay you. Average $0.30/word. Send queries to mojowire@motherjones.com.
http://motherjones.com

You can find guidelines for magazines stories at http://mother-jones.com/info/writers.guidelines.html

Ezines for the more esoterically minded

Anyone can create an ezine but generally they are produced by writers and editors who have developed their own websites. They understand the business of writing and spend a great deal of time, with their team, gathering together market news, interviews, and other writing-related material to include in the ezine. They are always on the look-out for the best websites, the most interesting ezines, forthcoming competitions, classes and discussion groups and mailing lists, and to some extent they rely on other writers to provide them with up-to-date information. There is little in the way of unhealthy competition amongst writers on the internet; there is a great deal of camaraderie and a willingness to share information with others. Sometimes it appears it is as if the writers who use the internet have a common voice; they share their words and their thoughts and ideas with millions of other writers world-wide.

Inscriptions

The weekly ezine for professional writers.
http://come.to/InscriptionsMirror
http://members.aol.com/maidenfate/Inscriptions.html

Netsurfer Books

A new ezine, featuring book reviews and recommendations. It is delivered to subscribers twice a month via email, and features HTML links to more information about each book, including the opportunity to purchase the book.

http://www.netsurf.com/nsb/

PageOne

Page One is a newsletter and website for all writers. Full of information, news, interviews and writing tips. Page One is FREE and you can subscribe by email to: Fictwri@aol.com

http://members.aol.com/FICTWRI/pageone.html

The Quill

An online resource and editorial centre for new writers.

http://www.thequill.com/

Ezines by genre

Whatever your preferred genre, you will find it on the internet. Remember, however, not to restrict yourself. You are on the look-out for all kinds of information about the writing scene on the internet in general but you are also interested in mainstream publishing and markets for your work. Look for useful writing tips, new websites or ezines, potential markets, new publishers, or a publisher that is seeking submissions, even a job, as you read and absorb the huge amount of information that you will find.

Of Ages Past

A monthly publication dedicated to historical fiction.

http://www.angelfire.com/il/ofagespast/index.html

Sequential Tart

An ezine covering the comics industry from a woman's point of view. Monthly format. Nicely irreverent.

http://www.sequentialtart.com

Screentalk

An ezine for screenwriters. Exclusive interviews with established screenwriters, producers, directors and actors from around the

world. In-depth articles about the craft and business of screenwriting.
http://www.screentalk.org

Cyber Age Adventures
The weekly ezine of the original super-hero fiction.
http://welcome.to/TheCyberAge

Gathering Darkness
An online horror magazine.
http://www.officextras.com/gdarkness/main.html

Mayhem Magazine
A new mystery/thriller magazine. *Mayhem* publishes fiction, artwork, comics, prose, reviews and other media dealing with thriller and mystery genres. A limited amount of true crime and related material may be published.
http://www.mediasi.com/chantingmonks/mayhem

UK-based online magazines

There aren't as many UK-based websites and related ezines to be found on the internet as there are on Canadian and US sites, but those that do exist are at the cutting edge of the industry. The websites listed below are exciting and they often provide the necessary information in clean and simple terms. Graphics are usually superb and although some of those listed are not just about writing – some of them cover the arts in general – they are not to be missed.

Dazed and Confused
A London-based music and fashion ezine with content that changes monthly. Provides reviews of all the new releases coming from the UK.
http://www.confused.co.uk

Peppermint Iguana Ezine
Interviews, reviews, articles, links and other weirdness.
http://www.iguana-net.demon.co.uk/

Bubblegum Internet
Ezine dedicated to low budget horror, sci fi and B-movies!
http://easyweb.easynet.co.uk/~cabrera/

e-tour

Interactive arts and culture ezine, based in East London but thinks globally. It includes a newsgroup, Java/Shockwave animations, and is very easy to navigate.

http://www.biblio.co.uk/e-tour/index.html

Submitting your work

Most ezines and magazines that advertise for work on the internet provide their own list of submission guidelines. Below are two examples of how this may appear:

New Writer's Magazine (a magazine in print)
http://www.newriters.com

NW is always looking for fresh new 'how-to' articles with a different slant. New trends in the traditional publishing and the new digital publishing field. Freelance writing is always welcomed. Buys One Time Rights.

NON-FICTION: An 'up close and personal' interview of a recognised or new author, preferably with photos, and all major 'in depth' articles on writing and the writing life. All such articles must be original and previously unpublished. 700–1,000 words. Payment on publication: $20–$40.

FICTION: Will publish a good fiction piece that has some sort of tie-in with the world of the new writer. Open to all styles and forms of expression. 700–800 words. Payment on publication: $20–$40.

POETRY: Humorous slant on writing life especially welcomed. Free verse, light verse and traditional. Submit maximum 3 poems. Length 8–20 lines. Payment on publication: $5 each poem.

Always remember to include an SASE (#10 envelope or whatever is required to return manuscript, with proper amount of postage), otherwise your submission or query may not be answered or it will be long delayed. No email submissions accepted.

Iagora (an online magazine)
GUIDELINES
(http://www.iagora.com/pages/html/about/guidelines.html):
Is a new virtual community/Webzine for international travel and is looking for submissions from freelance writers and everyday travellers. We run two types of articles: 1. Features (1,000–1,500 words)

can cover basically anything of interest to a wide global audience of sophisticated travellers (right now, mostly college students): politics, culture, food, religion. We especially welcome topics that will generate discussion in the Opinion box. Features can be written either as a personal narrative (1st person) or as a more traditional 3rd person article, but in either case should be analytical and preferably not too politically correct. We like to include, along with the centrepiece, a Sideshow (400–600 on a related topic) and/or a Profile (an interview with a relevant person). An extra fee is paid for each of these optional pieces. 2. Travel pieces (500–750 words) are travel anecdotes falling into two categories, "Culture Shock" (reactions to a different culture) and "Off the Beaten Path" (an unusual trip, destination, occupation). Because the articles are relatively short, keeping them centered around one particular theme or event generally works out best.

All articles will be published in four languages (French, German, Spanish and English). We are happy to accept submissions in any of these languages. Writers who are able to do their own translations will be paid an additional fee.

Fees for accepted articles:
Centerpiece: $40
Sideshow & Profile: $5
Travel piece: $20
Submit your piece to info@iagora.com.

These examples give you some idea of what format to expect when you start browsing through the multitude of online and mainstream magazines that you will find on the internet. However, if you are lazy, like most of us, you can try the Writers' Guidelines Database.

Writers' Guidelines Database
http://mav.net/guidelines

This is an incredibly informative site for writers; it lists hundreds of guidelines from paying markets. Freelance FAQ, links and a monthly newsletter. They also pay for advice pieces for writers. Visit http://mav.net/guidelines/ for the guidelines.

Make sure you follow the guidelines requested by ezines, as you would with mainstream magazines. Remember your submission is only one click away from internet oblivion.

Changing a mind set
Many people still believe that the quality of writing on the internet is not as good as it could be because anyone can get their work

published. However, these people miss the point that although the quality of writing does vary on the internet, users and readers of websites and web content still have pretty high standards. The beauty of the internet is that anyone can advertise or promote their work and no one else has to read it if they don't want to.

The question one must always ask is who has the right to decide whether content is of such poor quality that it should not be allowed on the internet? Many well-written books are not published because the authors fail to be in the right place at the right time and many poorly written books do get published. The internet has a thriving community of writers and allowing the good, bad and indifferent to mingle will raise the standard of the lowest and make the highest achieve even greater heights. Censorship of this nature does not belong on the internet.

And finally . . .

The internet can transform an inanimate object like a magazine into a totally interactive piece of media. It is possible for the writer to produce an article for an ezine about a particular pop star that will include a link to enable the reader to hear the pop star's music as they read. Reading an article can become an interactive, multimedia experience.

The writer who takes on this brief must be aware that writing for the web requires a certain style. Pieces must be shorter and more powerful and the writer must supply links to the source material. However, it is also true to say that many articles and stories found in ezines are not so technologically bound. And although writing for the internet does demand learning new skills, a few hours surfing the net will enable most writers to grasp what is required and to adapt their own particular style to the internet.

5

FICTION vs. NON-FICTION

Writing fiction for the internet

'I have seen the future and it works.' Lincoln Steffens

Writing fiction for the internet is certainly a new challenge for the writer. However, it is not as scary a business as some would like to make out – the same rules of writing apply online as they do in the mainstream. It has been suggested that the writer needs to acquire new skills to write fiction for the internet, that the writer must gain a new understanding of the 'grammar and syntax' of the internet to write successfully for it. This may be true for non-fiction but it is questionable where fiction is concerned. Fiction on the internet is very similar in style to print-based fiction at the moment, encompassing the good, the bad and the indifferent, and it would be foolish to be put off by such statements.

However, it is still important that the writer should develop entertaining, well-written stories or novels in order to stand any chance of success. If you are a skilled writer you will find the internet opens up a whole new world. If you are a novice writer, you will find the internet a paradise of information, helping you to avoid becoming isolated and ensuring that your knowledge base is permanently extended and updated.

Interactive fiction

However, there is one aspect of fiction on the internet that has perhaps re-defined the brief for many writers and that is 'interactive fiction'; in other words, fiction that is created online. This label also refers to a number of other sub-categories that seem to fall under the general title of 'interactive fiction', including collaborative fiction, tree fiction, hypertext novels and email fiction. If you want to explore the world of interactive fiction further, take a look at the following sites:

Hyperizons: Hypertext Fiction
An annotated bibliography of original hypertext fiction, criticism, and related sites. Much more than an interactive fiction site. If you don't

understand the concept of interactive fiction, then start here.
http://www.duke.edu/~mshumate/hyperfic.html

The Net

Internet fiction and digital narrative. The massive explosion of new types of internet fiction and digital narrative is a story in itself.

The BBC site provides a history of interactive fiction, where it has been and where it is likely to go in the future.
www.bbc.co.uk/the_net/3/1/item1.html

If you don't, no one else will . . .

In the print-based world there aren't many alternatives available to get published, whether you write fiction or non-fiction. You can self-publish quite easily these days but the promotional aspect can be quite daunting. You can pay huge amounts of your hard-earned money to a vanity publisher who will, as promised, produce your book but will probably not promote it adequately. Alternatively, you can create a website to promote yourself. Where else would it be possible to exhibit your material for next to nothing and have the prospect that many millions of people will have access to your work? This is the beauty of the internet: everyone can have a little slice.

It is true that promoting yourself on the internet is easier if you are offering a service of some kind, but many thousands of people have their own websites *entirely* dedicated to themselves and list them with all the major search engines – and who is to tell them they can't? Thousands of writers also have their own websites offering useful links and resources for other writers to use. If you don't feel confident enough initially to create a website then it is also possible to showcase your work on someone else's website. You will probably have to pay for this service, but it means that they get to do the technical bit and you can sit back and receive the accolades (Chapter 7).

The internet is, however, much more than an experiment in self-promotion, there are markets to be had, fortunes to be made, competitions to enter, online jobs to apply for and much more. It is a sad fact that non-fiction mostly pays better and is easier to write than fiction and many writers fund their fiction by selling their non-fiction to earn a living. After all, it pays bills and allows them to pursue the 'novel'. But the internet does at least allow the dedicated fiction writer the chance to broaden his or her horizons, perhaps providing a few opportunities that don't exist in the print-based media at the moment.

The key to success for the writer on the internet is to be as versatile as possible. If no one is interested in your fiction then perhaps consider trying non-fiction, and vice versa. If you make a name for yourself in one area you may be able to find success for other material that you have written. There are many avenues of possibility and you must have the confidence to pursue them; you must assess your own potential and skill level. It may seem a waste of your valuable time to stop writing fiction to pursue non-fiction but remember there is more than one way to skin a cat!

Submission guidelines for fiction

Just as submitting fiction to a print-based fiction publisher or to a magazine requires that you follow submission procedures, certain rules also apply when submitting your manuscript to a website, an online publisher or agent, or an ezine. Most editors when seeking submissions on the internet will give a clear list of their requirements and tell you exactly how you should submit material to them, whether via an email or snail mail. It is obviously in your best interests to observe them. However, it is always sensible to pay a visit to the site you are intending to target and take a good look at the content, style and presentation. You can then quickly pick up on the general tone and target audience of the website, just as you would for the print market, before you submit your work.

You really can have the best of both worlds on the internet because many editors seeking submissions don't necessarily want them for online purposes. So you can keep your eye on both the internet and the mainstream world of publishing at the same time – and benefit from both. It is important to remember that email submissions should be embedded into the body of the email rather than attached as a file. This means that you start writing an email offering your work to the chosen editor – including whatever details about the manuscript and yourself they have requested – and then you cut and copy your piece into the email itself, sign off and send. It's as simple as that. Each editor will, however, have their own preferences, so make sure you pay particular attention to individual guidelines. If for some reason you can't find submission guidelines anywhere on your target site, send a brief email to the editors. Tell them you are a freelance writer and that you are interested in writing for them. Ask them how they prefer to receive queries and, once you receive an answer, follow their requirements to the letter. Submit one or two pieces that you have written *specifically for them*, having already established their editorial slant from looking at the site.

Fiction Writers Connection

FWC is a membership organisation providing practical assistance and information to writers pursuing the craft of fiction. Among the benefits to members is a bi-monthly newsletter, *Fiction Writer's Guideline*.

http://www.fictionwriters.com/fwc/html/submissions.html

Images – Writer's Guidelines

Writer's Guidelines: Images is a forum for all types of writers. Covers movies, television, comic books, and other types of popular culture.

http://www.imagesjournal.com/writers.htm

The American Directory of Writer's Guidelines

As most sites on the internet are American this would probably be a good book to buy! If you can't beat 'em, join 'em.

http://www.graphic-design.com/Bookshelf/amguide.html

Manuscript format

Manuscript format varies from editor to editor, publication to publication, online or off. Usually, along with other guidelines, they should tell you how they want the manuscript presented, and this will probably be along the following lines:

Format: All entries must be in English and should be submitted in electronic format, either via email or as a text-only attachment. All text should be 12-point type, preferably in Times or Helvetica, single-spaced and left justified, with double spacing in-between paragraphs.

Or:

1. All submissions are preferred emailed in Word format, otherwise type-written on plain 8¹/₂ x 11-inch paper. Please be sure to include the Author Information/Story Cover Sheet with your submission.

2. Stories should be non-fiction, ranging in length between 1–4 pages of double-spaced copy.

3. Please provide information regarding the original author and the publication in which it appeared (see Author Information Sheet).

There are many websites that can help you prepare a manuscript in the correct manner to send either conventionally or electronically:

Word Museum
Full of 'Word Museum' news, articles, writing tips and fiction.
Offers a 24-hour chat service and a guestbook to sign. Also manuals for sale on topics such as manuscript format and other writing related topics.
http://wordmuseum.com/manuals.htm

Proper Book Manuscript Format
Compiled by American authors Lisa E. Brown and David Ward Davis. Produced courtesy of Aalida Press Book Publishers. An insight for British writers into US requirements.
http://www.aalida.com/wr1.htm

Proper Manuscript Format
A professional science fiction writer explains how to format a short story for submission to an editor. 'Cleverly disguised as a properly formatted manuscript!' he says.
http://www.shunn.net/format.html

Screenwriting Help
Information and resources for screenwriters. This site is dedicated to arming the screenwriter with the information and skills to compete with successful established screenwriters.
http://www.concentric.net/~pcbc/

How to write non-fiction for the internet

'Talent alone cannot make a writer.' Ralph Emerson

This statement is probably never truer than when used in reference to the internet; becoming a well-known, well paid writer takes tenacity, versatility and the ability to wear many different hats. There are, in reality, very few writers who can sit down, write a book, find a publisher and instant success, and then sit back for the rest of their lives reaping the benefits. For most writers it is hard and unrewarding work, occasionally interspersed with a moment of publishing joy. The rejection slips arrive with the return of manuscripts, what little money made is eaten up by overheads and most writers could never imagine the prospect of their writing supporting them.

The internet has alleviated this situation. Using facilities and opportunities that are available on the World Wide Web, writers can seek out markets and possibilities that simply don't exist in the print-based writing industry. They can seek employment as editors and proofreaders, freelance journalists and much more. They can command high payment for work or exhibit their work for all to see with a pride that is not felt so keenly when self-publishing. They can become versatile – writing material for CD-ROMs, offering their services to companies developing websites, writing book reviews, writing about the writing industry or trying their hands at new genres. All these possibilities and more are available to writers who are brave enough to venture into the future.

To be successful it is necessary to take full advantage of the concept behind the internet. For example, creating useful links within your text to highlight your most important points can add a new dimension to your writing. So, if you are writing an article on a topical matter, perhaps a political issue of the day, and you know that there are several other articles that highlight your own opinion in an online newspaper, you should make reference to these in your piece. This ability to take the reader to another site and to someone else's work can of course have its downside; they may never return to your piece if they get caught up in the subject matter and begin to explore more and more links. But rather than looking on this as a pitfall, you may well feel that this is the whole point of the internet. Your article in fact opened the door on the subject for the reader and took them to places that they would not have reached if they had simply been reading printed matter.

Writing requirements for the internet are much more specific than those for mainstream publishing. Articles may have to be shorter and more powerful. Writers are required to reach a new understanding of the written word. Much material on the internet is not necessarily structured in terms of a beginning, a middle and an end. Writing skills in the past have been based on a more logical approach, which enables a flow of thought from idea to idea. The writer on the internet, with the added dimension of hypertext links and search facilities that can link the piece of work to other sites or pieces of information, cannot assume that the reader will access the information in their article in any order. This non-structured approach means that readers can take the most effective route, depending on their knowledge, personal interest and expertise.

Writers used to presenting their ideas hierarchically may find it difficult to embrace the idea that writing for the internet often requires ideas that are self-contained within the piece of work they are writing. When writers are used to their ideas progressing and building on previous ideas, they may find it disconcerting to have to structure their work so that readers can choose to read some and to leave the rest. A beginner may feel the need to follow a link for further explanation of a topic; an expert may already have a detailed knowledge of the subject but may find that the gaps in his or her knowledge can be filled in by a link to a topic that will broaden their horizons. This method of writing, therefore, allows both the beginner and the expert to explore the subject in the way that suits their own knowledge base.

There may be no room for a beginning, a middle and an end on the internet, but there is plenty of room for writers to explore an entirely different world. The internet has opened new doors for writers in the sense that they are able to discover new and perhaps untapped areas of their own writing skills. It is also reassuring to note that some examples of writing on the internet appear to follow the same traditional, hierarchical structure as print-based media. Many articles have no hypertext links and they are structured with an old-fashioned beginning, middle and end. So, perhaps there is still room for the uninitiated after all!

Non-fiction guidelines

There are many non-fiction markets to be found on the internet, from sport and travel to cookery and health, even ghost-writing. Each subject area or topic will come with its own set of guidelines produced by the publication you are targeting; it is important that you find and follow them to the letter.

As with print-based non-fiction it is always better to write a piece for a particular purpose rather than to write the article or story first and then seek a market. This method will also increase your chances of success. Whatever your subject, you should always research the piece adequately, check facts, make sure it is suitable for its intended market and presented properly. This is particularly important on the internet; writing techniques will have to be adapted accordingly and this is where the writer's guidelines will become important.

Writers' Guidelines Database
http://mav.net/guidelines
This site will probably be listed in every chapter!

It is an incredibly informative site for writers; it has hundreds of guidelines from paying markets. Freelance FAQ, links and a monthly newsletter. They also pay for advice pieces for writers. Visit http://mav.net/guidelines/writing/theguide.shtml for their guidelines.

Finding a market

Non-fiction covers a broad spectrum of writing, as every writer knows, and non-fiction on the internet is no exception. It covers the same scale and scope of genres as the mainstream market does; from phone books to manuals, catalogues to directories, travel guides to How-To books, dictionaries to encyclopaedias, articles to biographies. All these examples of non-fiction can be found on the internet; either as online publications or mainstream markets looking for writers to contribute to the publication.

Many of the same principles apply to the mainstream. Put bluntly, non-fiction can be easier to write than fiction, it pays better, and it is easier to get published. Facts are routinely available on the internet and a few days' research will enable you to produce a good article. Pick your subject area and stick to it; getting your foot in the door applies as much on the internet as it does anywhere else. Once you have established a track record you can use it as a springboard into other areas of interest and extend your prospects into wider markets. Other points to keep in the front of your mind are:

- Find gaps in a market.
- Develop saleable ideas.
- Conduct market research.
- Avoid clichéd ideas.
- Don't repeat subjects that have already been done.

The next step is to find what you are looking for; finding non-fiction sites is not difficult and by now you should be a dab hand at using search engines, directories and links. Listed below are a number of sites that will help you find many non-fiction markets and hopefully lead you to websites specifically related to your own particular field of writing or interest.

Freelance Writing at Suite 101

This site is dedicated to any number of topics and has search and chat facilities. If you are searching for extra material or wondering what to write an article about, take a look. It is a huge site and anyone can join.

http://www.suite101.com/topics/page.cfm/1639

Non-Fiction Forum

Tips, questions, support, and resources for writing non-fiction. An extremely informative site, but why did they have to use those colours?

http://www.delphi.com/writenonfiction/

Freelance Success

Free newsletter. The site gives non-fiction writers the tools to earn a full-time living. Detailed market information and online writing classes.

Email freelance-success@usa.net or see
http://www.freelancesuccess.com

Writing Genres: Horror to Non-fiction

This site covers a variety of genres including non-fiction. General guide to a number of writing-related topics.

http://www.hukilau.com/yellowpage/db/writinggenreh-n.shtml

Creative Non-fiction

They state that Creative Non-fiction 'is the only literary magazine that focuses exclusively on the genre of creative non-fiction'. Whether this is true or not remains to be seen but it does include essays, memoirs, profiles, and book reviews, as well as interviews with prominent writers and commentary about the genre.

http://www.paintedrock.com/wharf/newsstand/writing.htm

Writing for the web

As web-writing is still in its infancy, there are no hard and fast 'rules' as yet. But these suggestions, culled from various internet sources, may give you food for thought:

- Try writing in the same way as you speak. This will make the work more concise and engaging.

- Use 'you' instead of 'I'.
- Sentences should be sharp and succinct, no more than 17 words long.
- Write short paragraphs. Remember to edit your work. Be brief.
- Give information in bite-sized pieces. People on the internet do not read in detail – they scan the page for clues, which may be textual, visual or aural.
- Use lots of sub-headings, dividing the piece by each separate idea.
- Use bullets.
- Avoid long narratives.

Always
- Spell- and grammar-check your work.
- Check your pages after uploading.
- Research editorial style well.
- Use hyphens sparingly.
- Use conventional spellings: use email, online, WWW, World Wide Web, website, web surfer, web page.

An eye on the future

As you may have discovered by now, the internet is constantly changing, and sometimes it can be hard to keep up with the new technology that appears almost daily. However, one of the simplest ways you can keep abreast is to predict future trends in your particular area of expertise. You can do this by keeping your eyes fixed firmly on the writing industry in general, read those ezines, take a look at the relevant newsgroups and websites, and keep up to date with the publishing industry both online and in the mainstream. Often success can be based on your ability to see into the future before anyone else – an old idea doesn't sell well, but a new one will be snapped up quickly.

In many senses we are already in the future as far as the internet is concerned and most writers are keen to keep up with developing trends. The most difficult step in getting online may be the first one. Once you have taken a good look round and surfed into as many writing sites as you have stamina for, you may begin to see where you can test the waters with your own writing. Whatever your interests or requirements are and whatever you seek from the internet, you are assured of finding it somewhere on the World Wide Web.

6

SURF'S UP!

The internet changes swiftly; one can bookmark a site in Netscape or select it as a Favourite in Internet Explorer and go back to take a closer look days or even hours later and find that it has been replaced by the words 'error: unable to locate URL'. This is an occupational hazard, so don't be put off. Most sites are there for the duration and it is not difficult to spot the quality ones – they are generally well constructed, offer a multitude of services under one roof and are run and constructed by professional writers dedicated to improving the writer's lot. Surfing the World Wide Web is easy, if confusing at times, but always tremendously liberating. The amount of information available at the touch of a key is invigorating, even a little scary; but it is this information that will improve your skills as a writer ... so, don't give in to the fear, do it anyway!

General information sites

There are so many writing-related sites on the internet, it would be impossible to list more that a small percentage of them. Here are a number of generally helpful sites to get you started.

Writer's Bookstore
Saves time trawling for books about writing. Offers many writing-related books for sale.
http://www.emergencepub.com/write01.htm

Writers World
Good site for writers. Lots of links, has members pages, lists of awards that are running and much more.
http://www.writersworld.net/

Inkspot
A comprehensive writing resource full of market information, tips on improving writing, articles, interviews with professional authors and editors, and more.
http://www.inkspot.com/

Journalism & Writers
Internet resources, dictionaries, grammar, and research facilities. Provides a point-and-click client interface for accessing various dictionary services on the internet. Linked to more than 400 dictionaries.
http://www.csj.org/journalism/jourwriters.htm

Current Issues in Web Usability
This site covers many aspects of web design, writing and multimedia issues.
http://www.useit.com/alertbox/

Online-Writing
Discussion list for those who write, edit and produce for the online medium. This site puts people across the world in touch with each other, and allows those writers who may live in the same areas to develop contacts.
http://www.planetarynews.com/networking.html

Good Documents
How to write for the intranet. A website that discusses how to create good business documents in the linked, on-screen environment of intranets and the internet.
http://www.gooddocuments.com

Literary Calendar
An almanac of literary events and people.
http://litcal.yasuda-u.ac.jp/LitCalendar.shtml

The Art of Writing
Good all-round site, offering tips, feature articles, markets and a free newsletter.
http://www.webcom.com/wordings/artofwrite/artofwriting.html

The Write Site
Includes links, tips, contests, quotes, exercises, ezines, and lists member bios, market listings, humour, a critiquing workshop, writers' conferences, online writers' groups, associations and organizations for writers, a character name guide, software for writers, news, book reviews, and a marketplace.
http://www.angelfire.com/al/thewritesite

Writing Now

This site manages to combine the best of both worlds by helping writers market their work to traditional and emerging media.
http://www.writingnow.com

E1.pub

News and resources on a host of interactive publishing issues.
http://www.pira.co.uk/IE

The Salt River Review

The Salt River Review believes in quality over quantity, and also tries to publish an interesting mix of writing. They especially welcome work from those who are new to web publishing.
http://www.mc.maricopa.edu/users/cervantes/SRR/

UK fiction and non-fiction sites

There are so many good quality US- and Canadian-based websites for writers on the internet that often you can be spoilt for choice. However, there aren't so many UK-based sites and those that are to be found tend to be general information sites covering a broad base of information about arts in the UK in general. The internet is truly versatile and perhaps the field of writing proves that as well as any. There aren't many mediums that allow for such a range of activities under one roof. A writer can apply for a job, submit material to an ezine, contact other writers, research an article, get guidelines for a particular market, or submit a book proposal. All this and more can be achieved in a day, an hour even.

Most UK sites are very elusive and can sometimes only be found through links from other more higher profile sites. It is worth taking a look at some of the professional organisations for writers on the internet, if only to see whether they offer links to any other UK sites.

With the arrival of free internet access this year, this may be a period of catch-up for the UK. Listed below are some of the fiction and non-fiction sites to be found based in the UK.

Live Literature Network

This is the Arts Council of England's website. It should be of interest to a broad spectrum of people in the publishing industry, who will find that they can use this forum as an effective resource tool.

You will also find a wide range of online and interactive events here, and they encourage you to use the site as a live venue.
http://www.liveliterature.net/

BBC Education — Web Wise
All you need to know about the internet and making the most of it.
http://www.bbc.co.uk/education/webwise

BBC Education
A lot of general information can be found on this site.
http://www.bbc.co.uk/education/home/today/

Computer Book Cafe
A site which includes a section for writers, with a Book Industry FAQ, a book proposal kit, tips on outlines, and other information.
http://www.studiob.com/

Mind's Eye Fiction
Ken Jenks is the editor-in-chief and owner of a paying market site for short stories on the internet. He is pleased to correspond with readers, writers, agents and publishers about online publishing.
http://tale.com/

Learned Information
Learned Information are event organisers and publishers for the information industry. Products include online information, the largest information event in the world and *Information World Review*, newspaper for the information industry. Learned Information also publish a series of IT Directories and electronic reference products based on these. Titles include the IT industry 'bibles' *The Computer Users' Year Book* and *The Software Users' Year Book*.
http://www.learned.co.uk

Digital Diaspora
Digital Diaspora is a network of artists, musicians and writers dedicated to fusing urban culture with new media. Live from Camden to the World Wide Web, Digital Diaspora will showcase a diverse array of established and emerging artists in contemporary popular culture collaborating online. Leading musicians, DJs and visual artists performing simultaneously at the cutting edge of multi-media technology.
http://aanemoss.com/diaspora

The Do-Not Press

The Do-Not Press, they claim, 'is to be found at the cutting-edge of modern publishing'. Home of the acclaimed Bloodlines crime and mystery series. Don't send anything to them unless you have taken a close look at their website and book list.
http://www.thedonotpress.co.uk/

Write-Link

Write-Link is a service to writers, whether professional or otherwise. They list writers' services, from publishers and manuscript services to competition lists and writers' groups.
http://www.linkcheck.co.uk/writelink/

Writer's Write

The Write Resource
NetGuide's Best of the Web commented that this site is 'A one-stop resource for professional writers.'
http://www.writerswrite.com/

Magazines and cultural ezines

Ezines and print-based magazines offer a good source of information and, more importantly, markets to target with your writing.

Estronet

This site is a clearinghouse for lots of women's ezines.
http://www.estronet.com

Salon Magazine

General interest electronic publication website and newsletter. Varied in style and content.
http://www.salon.com/

January Magazine

Culture, arts, fiction, non-fiction, cook-books, an assorted bag of writing-related info, reviews, etc.
http://www.januarymagazine.com

The New Pollution

The directory of Australian ezines (zines).
http://evolver.loud.org.au/nupoo/

Response Magazine
A monthly trade journal for the direct marketing business, including television, radio, the internet and print.
http://www.responsetv.com/topics/freelancer/freelancer.html

Lexikon
A varied and lively magazine for writers. Based in the UK but with an international focus, it includes practical advice, market and other news, reviews, competitions, poems, stories and a special section for children. Published quarterly, *Lexikon* is available on subscription in printed form as well as on cassette for the visually impaired. Material presented for publication is governed by terms of business and only non-fiction is included in the virtual version.
http://www.karoo.net/lexikon/index.htm

The Lighthouse
This encourages artists from different disciplines to explore the creative relationship between digital art practice and computer programming.
http://www.channel.org.uk/lighthouse/index.html

Poetry sites

Writers of poetry will know that getting poetry published in the print-based media is hard if not impossible these days. The internet is a wonderful platform from which poetry writers can launch their work.

Poetry Life
Hailed as Britain's sharpest poetry magazine. Articles on all aspects of the booming poetry scene in the UK and world wide, reviews, festivals, publishing, performance poetry, style and the politics of poetry.
http://freespace.virgin.net/poetry.life/

Poetry Daily
General poetry site.
http://www.poems.com/

Genre sites

Whatever your genre you will find a place for it on the internet. The World Wide Web has a place for everyone, and there are no real restrictions as to content on many of these sites.

Writers' Links
Links to sites covering such genres as horror, mysteries, romance and several links to magazine homepages; also information on the bad side of writing, scams etc.
http://www.geocities.com/Area51/Labyrinth/8584/writers.html

Romance Writers Homepage
New website built by and exclusively for Romance Writers.
http://www.simegen.com/out-t/romance/index.html

Lyrical Line Newsletter
Free newsletter for songwriters. To subscribe go to:
http://www.lyricalline.com/newsletter.html

Monthly Short Fiction Contest
Writers' Short Fiction Contest.
http://www.risingltd.com/Contest.html

The Thrilling Detective Web Site
Excellent site for all hard-boiled fiction scribblers or turners.
http://www.colba.net/~kvnsmith/thrillingdetective/

Zoetrope
Features outstanding new literary fiction by emerging and established authors.
http://www.zoetrope-stories.com/

The Semantic Rhyming Dictionary
A slick little online program that will find the rhyme for nearly any word.
http://www.link.cs.cmu.edu/cgi-bin/dougb/rhyme.cgi

The Mystery Review
Information and entertainment for mystery and suspense readers.
http://www.inline-online.com/mystery/contribute.html

Copyright information sites

The subject of copyright has been mentioned briefly. It should work in the same way on the internet as anywhere else, but, for a number of reasons too complicated to go into here, it doesn't. There are a few websites that deal with your rights and responsibilities, and you can take a look at them if you are concerned in any way. There are a number of things you can do to protect your copyright if you are worried. It is a thorny problem and no doubt until the internet is brought under 'copyright' control it will continue to dog certain sections of the media.

A Novice Writer's Guide to Rights
By Claire White; part of the 'Writers Write' website. This site will give you some idea of where you and your work stand as a writer and explains some of those technical terms that writers tend to ignore.
http://www.writerswrite.com/journal/dec97/cew3.htm

PubLaw Update
A free information service provided to the publishing community by The Publishing Law Center. This service consists of periodic mailings of articles, which concern publishing law (copyright, trademarks, contracts, and other issues involving the protection of intellectual property rights), as well as articles that can help publishers with the business of running a profitable publishing company.
http://www.publaw.com
Email at: info@publaw.com

For love or money

Some writers on the internet say that they won't write anything for under a $1 a word; and maybe they don't have to, but this is not the reality for most writers. There are many high-paying markets on the internet, but most pay quite modestly. The reality is that a writer may well scoop some very well-paid work, but to continue working consistently they will have to accept other work that is not so highly paid. Whether you are writing for love or money or both, or you are writing fiction as opposed to non-fiction you need to make sure your work follows the guidelines set down by your particular market.

Useful Information for Authors
Lots of information to be found here. Internet links, online bookstore and FAQ section.
http://home.clara.net/paulm/writing.html

Ink Spot's Market Info for Writers
List of markets, occasionally high-paying ones.
On the site are articles on writing, a board for networking, etc.
http://www.inkspot.com/bt/market/

Online Writer's Guidelines
Guidelines to various magazines and markets.
http://www.geocities.com/Athens/Forum/6682/guidelines.html

Writer's Digest
If you've been writing for any length of time, you know WD. They also have a nice guidelines database on board the web now.
http://www.writersdigest.com/

Library and reference sites

As you would expect there are many specialised library sites on the internet. Remember that some of these libraries do actually exist! They are not all virtual creations, some deal in real books and with real people; they even have real librarians. But the majority are simply libraries who have websites and who can be contacted via email if you wish. If you are having trouble researching a particular subject, find a good library and email your request directly to them.

Stumpers
This is a mailing list for research librarians, so you can tap in directly to their knowledge if you choose.
http://www.cuis.edu/~stumpers/

The World Ezine Library
If you are looking for a specific market to target you may find it at this website and more.
http://www.ezinelibrary.com/cgi/lib/members/EC18.html

1st Books Library
A good site for downloading virtual books.
http://www.1stBooks.com

Britannica Online
Encyclopedia Britannica on the internet. Demo and subscription info.
http://www.eb.com/

British Library
The British Library's online information server.
http://portico.bl.uk/

The National Bibliographic Service
http://opac97.bl.uk/

Commonwealth Literature Library
This free service, partially funded by sponsorship from **Amazon.co.uk**, will allow you to find out what material is held in the major Reference and Document Supply collections of the British Library. In many cases it will also be possible to request copies of document supply material from the Library's Document Supply Centre (BLDSC) at Boston Spa.
http://www.commonwealth.org.uk/

Look Dictionaries
A list of well over 200 online dictionaries and glossaries, some dealing with pretty esoteric subject matter including castles, cooking and oncology.
http://www.onelook.com/browse.shtml

Public Libraries
Here you will find a linked list to more than 500 libraries.
http://sjcpl.lib.in.us/homepage/PublicLibraries/PubLibSrvsGpher - WWW.html#wwwsrv.

The Electronic Library
This site is good for students and families. Thirty days' free access ...
http://www.elibrary.com/

Writers' groups

There is a full list of writers' circles and assorted writers' groups on the author.co.uk website at http://www.author.co.uk.

Software for writers

Make of these what you will!

The Writer's Software Companion
An award-winning CD by *Writer's Digest*'s Nancy Kress which rapidly accelerates writing/learning process. Includes SOFTWARE DREAMPACK FOR WRITERS, 57 free/shareware writers' programs, from brain trainers to time-savers and writing coaches. Free downloads and extras:
http://www.novalearn.com/sites/ink.htm

Storycraft Writer's Software
The popular story-creation software for writing every type of fiction. Also, online writing program taught by Storycraft's inventor.
http://www.storycraft-soft.com

SwiftTrack for Manuscripts
Tracks submissions, income, expenses. All information on screen at once. Fast data entry via pick lists. Response timers. Due date alarms. Print preview for reports. Email SwiftTech@compuserve.com or see http://ourworld.compuserve.com/homepages/SwiftTech/ to download.

Regional arts boards

Many writing-related organisations list their services with regional arts boards and they can be a huge source of information for writers, including local facilities, events and writing courses available around the country.

Regional Arts Pages
Includes a web and email directory, arts news, map of regions, community arts information, database of information sheets and access for the visually impaired. It also provides links to other regional arts boards around the UK.
http://www.arts.org.uk/

The Arts Council of England
The national funding body for the arts in England. It is responsible for developing, sustaining and promoting the arts through the distribution of public money from central government and the revenue generated

by the National Lottery. The Arts Council exists to help people enjoy the arts by supporting drama, music, dance and touring companies, contemporary art galleries and exhibitions, film and literature projects.
http://www.artscouncil.org.uk/ACEindex.html

The Department for Culture, Media and Sport
The central UK government department responsible for Government policy on the arts, sport and recreation, the National Lottery, libraries, museums and galleries, export licensing of cultural goods, broadcasting, film, press freedom and regulation, the built heritage, the royal estate and tourism. It also has responsibility for royal parks and palaces through two executive agencies, Royal Parks and the Historic Royal Palaces Agency, and for the Government Art Collection. It represents the UK's interests in various international forums. Many of its activities are carried out via Non-Departmental Public Bodies (NDPBs) and public corporations.
http://www.culture.gov.uk/ARTS.HTM

Arts Council of New Zealand Toi Aotearoa
Creative New Zealand's role is to promote the arts of the country, support artists and encourage more New Zealanders to enjoy the arts. They do this by funding a wide range of projects by artists and arts organisations, advocating for the arts, and undertaking initiatives and research projects.
http://www.creativenz.govt.nz/cnz/what/index.html

The Art Link
This site offers an impressive range of links, including the ADAM Project (Art, design, architecture and media resources on the internet, including a search facility). Art Crimes (graffiti) Art Services & Circa Arts and cultural pages from Ireland. Online art gallery. Arts in Scotland. An online communications service. Arts Wire is a service mark of the New York Foundation for the Arts. British Federation of Festivals for Music, Dance and Speech. Chinese Arts Network (UK). Chinese artists living and working in Britain. Department of National Heritage. Rural American b&w photography. Edinburgh's Fringe Festival and WorldWide Arts Resources which includes thousands of arts links and much more.
http://www.thedirectory.co.uk/

The British Council – USA – Arts and culture

Information about Britain – arts and culture. Visit the British Council's 'Arts' home page. Government and official bodies, Department for Culture, Media and Sport. The Millennium Commission. Many links to the British art scene and more.
http://www.britcoun.org/usa/usabrit1.htm

Professional organisations on the internet

It is always important to keep an eye on the writing industry's professional status and your role within it. You may well be advised to join the professional organisation related to your field; this may help you with networking, jobs and information vital to the progression of your career.

Prof Net

A collaborative of 6,000 public relations professionals linked by the internet to give journalists and authors convenient access to expert sources. They have a direct link to 6,000 news and information officers at colleges and universities, corporations, think tanks, national labs, medical centres, non-profits, and PR agencies.
http://www.profnet.com

The Authors' Licensing and Collection Agency

ALCS was founded in 1977 to enable writers to receive fees that are uniquely or more effectively handled collectively. But this site is not just to do with the administrative side of collecting fees for writers, it offers a broad base of information too. You can join as an ordinary member for free. It provides a forum for discussion, resources and links to many other sites of interest. They have divided their categories up into user friendly divisions for easy navigation.
http://www.alcs.co.uk/

Internet Free Press

A particularly forward thinking site. The aim of the internet Free-Press is to get all writers who are interested in 'creating the electronic publishing revolution' to share their ideas and expertise. Internet Free-Press can serve as a meeting place, a library, and a market place for exchange and trade.
http://www.free-press.com/

International Women's Writing Guild
The International Women's Writing Guild is a network for the personal and professional empowerment of women through writing.
http://user.aol.com/fireworxs/WRITERS.html

Internet Press Guild
This is a brilliant site for writers venturing on to the internet for the first time, and could possibly teach an old dog new tricks as well. Discusses internet journalism and offers helpful tips to get you started.
http://www.netpress.org/index.html

The European Federation of Freelance Writers
Membership of the European Federation of Freelance Writers is open to freelance journalists, feature writers and authors throughout Europe. The EFFW provides professional support to all members of the writing profession but specifically freelance or part-time writers, freelance or part-time journalists, authors (fiction and non-fiction), trade and technical writers and authors of scientific papers.
http://www.eurofed.org/

7

MARKETING AND PROMOTING YOUR WORK

Looking back to see forward

Traditionally, marketing and promoting a book goes hand in hand with a publishing contract. The publishers do the promoting and marketing of your work for you, through book fairs, radio, newspapers, pre-release parties, review copies, flyers, listings and press releases, etc. The same applies when you self-publish a book, except you have to do the legwork. If you fail to promote your work adequately, it will probably fail.

The marketing and promotional side of the publishing industry are probably the two most important factors involved in the success of any work; we have all seen the advertisements in the paper and read the reviews. They don't happen by accident. The editors, reviewers and radio stations do not go to the author or the publisher to ask them when they are going to publish something, the publishers seek the publicity from them. Publicity is the key to success. The advertising, sales, distribution and promotion of a novel needs careful orchestration and must be done at the right time and to the right people.

The internet is different. If you have internet access you would be crazy not to promote yourself. The first major success story for one particular writer, Nan McCarthy, began when she self-published her novel and sold it via the internet. She sold 2,000 copies – not a great deal in traditional publishing terms, but this led to a mainstream deal with a print-based publisher. She then marketed her second novel by emailing all those people who had visited her website and 70 per cent of those placed orders.

The other alternative for writers on the internet is to by-pass the book completely and simply e-publish your work (Chapter 11). This means that you would simply provide the novel or non-fiction work on disk to an electronic-publisher to put on their website. They would then be responsible for promoting your work on their site by making it available for people to download, for a fee, from that site. This type of arrangement is becoming increasingly common and popular on the internet because most e-publishers pay royalties to writers in the same way as print-based publishers. At present e-publishers are having great success with the classics; authors such as Austen and Shakespeare are being downloaded from these sites at a brisk rate and it shouldn't be long before other authors find the same success. Submission procedures are similar to those for a print-based publisher, although you should make initial enquiries by email to establish the exact form this takes. Individual e-publishers may vary in their submission procedures as do mainstream publishers.

Promoting yourself as a writer

Promoting oneself as a writer is particularly hard if you are not published either in the mainstream or on the internet. No one knows who you are and no one has seen or read your work and you have no track record. So the idea of self-publishing (or e-publishing) your manuscript as a promotional tool is a sound one for any writer, whether you have a website or not. For a relatively small outlay you can have fifty copies of your novel – or non-fiction title – published and use the copies to promote yourself and your work. This means that your promotional quest may well begin by following the well-trodden traditional route of plugging a book.

This type of self-promotion will involve you in the following tasks:

- sending review copies to literary editors of newspaper and writing magazines
- submitting press releases to the local radio in your area asking them if they would be interested in talking to you; the same for local newspapers
- approaching local bookshops to see if they would be interested in taking a few copies of your book.
- sending out flyers
- contacting publishers who might be interested in looking at your work in its published form

The point to remember here is that while you are promoting yourself in this more traditional way you can also promote the fact that you have a website where samples of your work can be seen, and where interested parties can download complete copies of your work for a fee or alternatively buy a hard copy of your book.

Make sure that you list your email address and the URL of your website wherever possible. Sell yourself as a writer who can utilise both traditional marketing and promotional tools and the new technology – such as the internet – with equal ease.

You must be willing to push yourself forward into the limelight. You must also try to be as versatile as you can. Try writing short stories or articles and submit them to ezines or websites that are looking for content. The more credits in terms of published material you can get under your belt the more chance you will have of getting your work known and if this also means utilising avenues that are traditionally used for marketing goods and services then so be it. List any publishing success you have with ezines and newsletters that have an appropriate advertising section.

Obviously the first step to promoting yourself on the internet is to secure a web presence. Set up a website, and start marketing your work from it (see Chapters 8 and 9). Once you have done this you can begin to list the title and URL of the website with as many search engines, other writing-related websites and organisations as you can find on the internet. Wherever you come across 'add a site' on the internet, take it as an invitation to do exactly that and list your URL. This type of advertising on the internet is usually free and you should take advantage of the opportunity.

However, getting a website and promoting your work on it is only half the battle. If you are really serious about being a writer then getting published is probably your ultimate aim and you must submit your work regularly in whatever form that is required. If you write non-fiction articles, or short stories, or if you have written a novel, then the most important thing you need to do is submit them to magazines or publishers, whether online or not. As a writer who can utilise both traditional and electronic submission tactics you should be at an advantage.

Marketing your work on the internet

Sometimes, the writer needs to use techniques that may seem to be alien to the art of writing. Marketing is not a word that most writers feel comfortable about or even understand. They usually link it to goods and services. But since the internet is almost entirely US based and since Americans are so good at selling themselves it is necessary for other writers from other countries to learn from them and to see themselves as a commodity that can be marketed and sold. Once this has been done writers can adapt traditional marketing methods to suit their own needs.

Many writers will blanch at the idea of selling themselves; they equate it with selling their soul to the devil and feel that their work will be compromised if they get their hands dirty in this way. These techniques do not sit easily with the English mentality. However, to compete, this is what must be done.

Marketing on the internet must be considered as a separate process to that of mainstream marketing. It is not being utilised to the full at present; people who market their goods and services on the internet tend to create a homepage and leave it at that.

If you can use both internet and mainstream marketing, you will have the best of both worlds. But the first step to successful marketing on the internet is to recognise what is possible and to ignore what has gone before. The internet is a medium that can be used in any way you want and that means you don't always have to follow in someone else's footsteps or tread the conventional route. Sometimes to get the best out of something you have to think laterally.

Publishers' Marketing Association Newsletter Online

PMA Newsletter Online. This online version of the *PMA Newsletter* features selected articles about the book publishing industry, including legal questions, marketing issues, PMA events, business tips and advice, along with other important and/or ...

http://www.pma-online.com/

Résumé /CV

Sending out a résumé or CV with a sample of your work is an easy and effective way of securing work and marketing yourself at the same time. You can use a résumé to apply for a specific job or simply send it with a polite enquiry seeking work. A résumé can be sent either by conventional mail or by email, and whichever way it is sent it may put you on the records of the magazine or ezine you have targeted. If a suitable writing job comes up they may think of you.

Have a résumé prepared and select an appropriate sample of your work ready to send to a prospective editor if you are applying for a writing job or just making an enquiry about openings.

An effective résumé does not necessarily rely on a writer's track record. If you enclose a strong piece of writing which appeals to the editor then it won't matter to them or anyone else that you have not been published before. Don't let the fact that you have not had any work published restrict your search for writing jobs and try to be as confident as possible when you are seeking work. Confidence is always the key; if you think you can do it then others will tend to believe you.

Proposals

Proposals can be sent out by email to online publishers in the same way as you would submit them to print-based publishers. A proposal generally includes an outline of the complete book, the synopsis (which is really the sales pitch) and a covering letter. At this stage there is no need to write the book, in most cases you should not have written the book before sending out a proposal. The editor may wish you to take a slightly different slant on the topic than you had intended and you may have to re-write the work. You can of course write a few chapters while the editor is considering your proposal, in case he asks to see a sample of your work.

Posting
There are many writing websites that allow prospective job seekers to post details of themselves and the type of work they are looking for on their sites. It would seem a shame not to take advantage of a free chance to advertise yourself on the internet.

Set up your own website
This is dealt with in detail in the next chapter. (If we were on the web, I would provide a hypertext link here!)

If you do not feel confident or knowledgeable enough to create you own website then engage someone who can, rather than risk having a poor site which will reflect badly on you. Some web designers are expensive but there are cheaper ones around and everyone these days knows someone who is a computer expert. Find them and exploit them.

Rising Sun Web Design
A small outfit that will put the novice at ease.
Email: risingsun@claramail.com

Mailing lists and newsletters
Consider creating your own newsletter. Join a service such as **ListBot.com**. This is a site that will allow you to create a mailing list. Users who visit your site simply supply their email in a box provided by ListBot and then click to join the mailing list. ListBot allow you, as the

owner of the website, to manage the mailing list and send messages to any user who has joined from the ListBot site for no fee. They also allow you to ask certain information of the people who join the mailing list: age, occupation, etc. – and this will give you some idea of the type of people visiting your site. This gives you a direct line of contact with people who are interested in your work. It means that you can inform them that you have published a book or written an article that they can read, either by going to your site or visiting the site where it is published.

Alternatively you can create an ezine of your own; gather interesting writing-related material together, let other people advertise their work, publish your own work and that of other writers, and use this as a promotional tool. Just make sure that the layout is clear and concise, that the text is grammatically correct and readable, and make sure that you entertain the reader.

Banner adverts

Consider using banner ads to advertise your site and your work. The banner ad is simply the internet's version of a billboard. Banner ads allow you to get a message across in clear and simple terms and is usually emblazoned across the top of a search engine, or a writing-related website. The internet user, if interested, can use it as a link directly to your site. The banner ad should include your web address (URL) and a simple but bold statement, even an illustration; something that is going to attract attention, something quirky or even funny can fit the bill, to make the user want to take a closer look. Banner ads are not cheap and they are priced to reflect the number of exposures they will receive. So a banner ad on the search engine Yahoo UK will cost a considerable sum because it will attract huge number of visitors. However, there are good deals to be had. Remember that banner ads are ideal for tapping into the traffic already visiting the site. The web has a huge amount of advertising space up for grabs.

Charles Kessler & Associates

Provide online marketing, consulting, outbound marketing services, ad banner placement Online book promotion offers resources and services for marketing and promoting your book online.
http://www.bookpromotion.com/services.htm

Radio and newspapers

Many radio and newspaper are online and you must tap into these resources as well. Use their resources in the same way as you would use traditional media outlets. Send them press releases or proposals for a discussion, look for radio stations that have slots for one-off pieces – such as Radio 4's Thought for the Day' or Channel 4's 'Video Nation' – write an article or review a book for the literary section of a newspaper. You will need to find out which radio or TV station or newspaper would be amenable to receiving writing-related copy and the list below will provide you with a starting point from which to launch yourself into the world of the media online.

Online media contacts
Ezine Collections by Nerd World Media
Magazines are compiled under 50 subject headings from 'Arts & Entertainment' to 'Paranormal Science to Youth'. Each listed magazine is a hyperlink that will jump you to their website. A two- or three-line description helps with your selection. A search facility will help you to narrow down your list.
http://www.nerdworld.com/users/dstein/nw30.html

IS/OOP Group's Online Magazine Zine Thing
The IS/OOP Group has compiled 45 indexes of ezines. An accompanying synopsis describes each of the periodicals. You can visit another magazine's website by clicking on its hypertext link. You'll have to fill out their guest form before you can look at their contents page.
http://www.online-magazine.com/

The MIT List of Radio Stations on the Internet
MIT claims the most comprehensive list of internet radio sites. List keeper Theodore Young claims over 2,000 internet radio stations. Young has not made a practice of describing the stations by format such as Rock & Roll, News, or Talk Radio.
http://wmbr.mit.edu/stations/list.html

BRS Radio Directory
BRS also claims the most comprehensive list of internet radio stations. BRS has categorised stations by call letters, cybercasters' names, states, formats, non-commercial, and international.
http://www.brsradio.com/stations/index.html

Newspapers Online
A comprehensive list of online newspapers across the world.
http://www.newspapers.com/

Public Sector Intelligence Bulletin

News and information service on UK electronic government, tele-democracy and the information society. The Bulletin is an independent publication, aimed at internet users across government, local government, the social sector and their private sector partners.
http://www.iib.com

Press Association

Up-to-the-minute news and views. UK based.
http://www.pa.press.net/

Online resources for writers

There are many resources for writers on the internet that will help you to promote and market your work. Again, you have to find them and use them for your own purposes, and the only way to do this is to trawl the internet. It can be time-consuming and confusing but if you bookmark those websites that you find particularly informative you can go back to them and take a longer, closer look.

You are a writer and it would be sensible to use writing-related websites to promote or market your work. But do consider expanding your horizons to take in areas that will attract broad general attention. Cultural ezines, arts boards, writers clubs, and ezines that discuss developing marketing trends on the internet are areas that may be neglected by the writing fraternity and they would benefit from more writing-related input.

The Professional Writer's Source

Kaye Vivian, a proposals writer, provides a number of electronic resources for professional writers.
http://www.cloud9.net/~kvivian/

America Online Writer's Club

The Writer's Club features the following areas: author interviews, writing tips, genre information, 'meet the writers', writers' chat, reference area, and a message board. Two unique sections are the mentor program and writers' search. The latter allows you to look for archived articles using search terms.
http://www.writersclub.com

Marketing
The news magazine of the internet economy.
http://www.thestandard.com/

IdeaMarketers
A writer-publisher matching service.
http://www.ideamarketers.com/

Feed
Techno-biased cultural monthly.
http://www.feedmag.com

Hot-wired
The electronic spin-off from *Wired* magazine.
http://www.hotwired.com

Slate
The Microsoft sponsored cybermag.
http://www.slate.com

Word
A daily updated cultural ezine.
http://www.word.com

The good news

Good marketing involves good communication. This is good news for the writer because that is what writing is all about. Marketing is simply the art of communicating what you have to offer and convincing the reader/editor that they should purchase your book/article/proposal. You must sell yourself and your work with equal vigour.

As a writer with good communication skills, you should be able to develop a compelling message to sell yourself and your work. You may have to consider learning some skills in this. The synopsis is a good example. Many writers fall at the first post because they have not written a clear and concise synopsis. Your synopsis is your sales pitch. It will persuade the editor not only that you are a skilled writer but that the novel or work you are proposing is compelling enough to be considered. The same principle applies to the proposal and the résumé. They need to be compelling enough or you will fall at the first hurdle.

8

CREATING A WEBSITE

Having your own website can bring several advantages but on its own it is not much more effective than a scarecrow standing in a field. It needs care and attention if you are to reap rewards. Too many sites open with a huge graphic which takes several minutes to load. It then leaves the visitor wondering what the site is about, and how they can reach the pages it contains. Moving images or scrolling text are often over-used at the expense of content.

You have less than six seconds to make an impression, and no time at all if your page takes too long to load. Visitors to websites make a decision in seconds; to stay or to blow! Make them wait too long for the page to appear, and they will be gone. You are just a click away from oblivion.

Content of the site

What will you put on the site? Hopefully not pictures of the kids and a list of your favourite films. Leave those for personal pages kept on another site. This website is for your business of writing. The opening page could contain your picture, a short biography and a description of your work. The style should be friendly and conversational. Try to be yourself. You are trying to establish a few personal contacts, people with whom you can form a close business relationship. Formality does not work on the web and any form of deceit will be quickly recognised. Your online résumé is the clearest way to show the world your writing skills.

The opening page must open quickly, showing immediately what the rest of the site is about and providing links to specific areas of interest. Address the audience personally. Only one person is looking at the page at any time. Try to imagine arriving at the opening page with no idea of what the site contains and provide new visitors with an immediate explanation. The website can be used for a variety of purposes. You may have a manuscript to sell. One approach may be to present the synopsis on one page, with another showing a sample chapter; then you could include some suggestions about possible markets. Look at the whole package from the publisher's viewpoint. Do you have a saleable product? Could they make money from your work?

Include another area on the site for past work. Make sure that you have the permission of the copyright holder before displaying the actual text and then use the site to promote your last book, or to display out-of-copyright articles, adding press comments and any other related material. Copyright of electronic material is the subject of considerable debate. It is possible to watermark text in much the same way as graphic images. Ted Nelson, of hypermedia fame, suggests that all material on the web should carry an acknowledgement of its source; he even suggests that only links to the copyright owner's site should be tolerated. There are dangers as the material you place on your site is in the public domain and can easily be copied. Each page should carry the © **copyright sign**, together with the year of creation and the writer's name. In the UK that protection remains until 70 years after the death of the author. Join the **Authors Licensing & Copyright Society**; they provide many useful services.

Keep it simple. The front page should load quickly and contain clear information. Look at the **Yahoo** search engine pages. They load fast and they provide plenty of links that are easily understandable. Avoid spinning Java, Applets, huge graphics and confusing jazzy designs. The Yahoo site provides straightforward information with very few graphics (just six) and 'easy to understand' links. There is space elsewhere on the site to include complex designs. Always warn users if a graphic lies behind the next link that may take some time to load.

This chapter is not a guide to the mechanics of web page design; if you want that you will find an increasing collection of good books and plenty of useful contacts on the internet. Start by subscribing to a mailing list such as http://www.webreference.com/. They will send you a regular ezine full of tips and useful information.

The World Wide Web communicates using **http (hypertext transfer protocol)** which, in turn, uses a programming language called **HTML (hypertext mark-up language)**. HTML is fairly easy to learn. If you open the View, Source windows on your browser the HTML code that has been used to create the page on your screen will be revealed.

Most word processing programs allow you to create pages in HTML. You have to do very little except set out the page in the way you wish, then save the file to disk, making sure that the file format is HTM or HTML (they are the same). A professional approach is to use a good HTML editor, such as **Corel Webmaster**, **Hot Boot**, or a vendor-specific program such as **MS Front Page**. A good internet magazine, such as **Internet Works**, will carry reviews of these programs. Look for a program that provides good site management features. Make sure it will check your links effectively, reveal orphan pages and show how many levels there are in your site.

Most of these programs will help you gently through the process of creating a web page. It is not really difficult, although to begin with it may be time consuming. HTML can be written using any basic text editor, although that does require great care to ensure that all the programming symbols are included. Perseverance will pay dividends; open the source code of the good pages found as you surf the web. Look at the way the page is constructed and adapt those ideas on your own pages.

The opening page on your website is normally called the **homepage.** As with every other page on your site it is really an HTML file created and saved in a folder on your own computer. This is then transferred to the computer of your **internet service provider,** normally using an **ftp program (file transfer protocol)** to transfer the files. Ftp programs are usually included within web creation programs, or they can be purchased separately or may be provided by the internet service provider. Homepage files should be named either *homepage.htm* or *index.html* so that when a surfer types in the **URL (Unique Reference Locator)**, such as http://www.your-site.co.uk in the address line of their browser they will arrive at your homepage. The other pages can have any name but require the full file name, with **.htm** or **.html** within the URL, such as http://www.yoursite.co.uk/nextpage.htm.

The website needs to present a flavour of its own, to have a distinctive presence which comes through on every page of your site. There are some basic rules that beginners should follow.

Keep the page design simple
This cannot be repeated often enough. Most people are using fairly old computer equipment to access the web. The technology moves very quickly and it is impossible to keep abreast. Home users are likely to have better equipment than schools and businesses. Assume that most users are lagging well behind current technology standards. A large number of users will browse using the text-only facility, choosing not to see the latest gimmicks. Most browsers enable users to switch off several facilities, allowing access to the web with the graphics, sound and video switched off. This can be very useful when

searching for information. Most users have relatively poor connections to the internet. The biggest complaint about the net is the slowness of connecting to sites. Switching off graphics, which slow down the speed of loading a page, can make a dramatic difference. Users can then move much more quickly around the web, rapidly downloading pages.

Remember also that there are only a few colours that can be relied upon to reproduce accurately on other computers. The colours shown on the originator's computer screen may look different elsewhere. To make matters worse the most widely used internet browsers, **MS Internet Explorer** and **Netscape Navigator,** have different palettes, so choose your colours with care. Page design needs to work to the simplest format, taking into account all the variations that the page may find as it scoots around the web, being loaded on to many different types of computers.

Test each page design on a variety of browsers, especially Netscape Navigator (the most popular browser in use at present) and Microsoft's Explorer. VDU monitors vary in size and quality and pages should be designed to allow most users to view the pages properly. Setting the screen window size to fit a 21" monitor would mean that those with the most common monitors found – 14" or 15" – will miss part of the picture. Setting the window size to 600 x 800 pixels will allow most users a readable display.

Concentrate on fast download times

Keep page file sizes small, if possible below 20 Kb, and certainly below 40 Kb. A page of that size can contain a lot of text, perhaps 5,000 words. The problems arise when graphics, audio or video files are included. A small (2" square) picture – maybe the front cover of your book – can take up a lot of file space. Website creation software often shows the load time for pages. Set it to show the load time for a 28.8 Kb modem and experiment to gain the quickest upload time possible.

Keep graphic files small

Most internet graphics do not require high resolution; 72 dpi (dots per inch) is sufficient to view pictures easily onscreen. The internet provides some help; http://www.netmechanic.com will process a graphic and then display it in a variety of formats, allowing you to choose the one that displays the image clearly, yet has the smallest file size. Valuable free resources such as these can dramatically improve the operation of your site as the graphics will look their best, and will download quickly.

Remember content is king

Make your pages interesting and relevant to site visitors and keep them up to date. The primary purpose of a website may be to promote your work but the culture of the internet demands that users also obtain useful information. Include links to useful sites that provide advice or pertinent information. Always remember that visitors come to the site for what you offer them. This site is for them, not for you. Try to create a theme by which the site is known. If you are a romantic novelist the site could include a list of romance novels, links to suitable romance websites and information about the structure of such novels. Consider adding your own best-seller list or inviting visitors to suggest their own lists of favourites, which you then can post to the site. Add interest and variety.

Keep it easy to use

Use the opening page to describe the purpose of the site briefly and have a navigation bar that will take visitors quickly to other pages. The homepage must tell your story, quickly and efficiently, with easy-to-understand links to the other pages. Tinkling bells and other sophisticated devices can come much later, on other pages.

Update frequently

Change the content as often as you can. Once a day is not excessive, although it may be unrealistic. Potentially the site could receive many visitors every day, and they should be encouraged to return. Forming personal relationships with site visitors will bring the greatest rewards. You are not selling hamburgers or fizzy drinks to millions; you are trying to establish close ties with a small group with whom you will do business. Archive old material, making it available for all to see, once again providing clear links to those pages.

Make it fun

OK, you want to sell your writing but the website should offer the visitor much more than that. One writer created an online quiz based on the plot of her historical novel. She used the background material gathered for her book, and displayed it on separate pages, as answers to the series of questions she asked of site visitors. Joke pages are popular, and it is easy to provide crosswords or word puzzles – the software to help you to create such programs can be bought quite cheaply. Mention your hobbies and pastimes, not 'here is a picture of me and my dog and we go walkies' but useful information such as the research or background material that you have accumulated. This will throw up lots of snippets, many of which could find a place on your site.

Make buying easy

If you are selling a book, make it easy to buy online. If possible accept credit card payment online. UK banks are still not relaxed about internet commerce but that will change. Within a few years most business-to-business transactions will take place over the internet. Your bank need not be based in this country and the internet itself is not geographically dependent. A variety of payment systems should be offered. Credit card payments are easy but also provide online order forms that can be emailed or faxed to your distributor. If you have more than one book, then add a shopping trolley so that items can be marked for purchase as the user moves around. Show addresses, telephone, fax, email and website addresses clearly and on every page. Provide links to online book-stores like **Internet Bookshop** and **Amazon** who will pay a small commission for every book sold as a result of links to their sites. Consider making text available online, selling it using **Pay2See** or some other agency. Be convenient and helpful. When clients want to give you money, help them.

Chat, message boards and ezines

Link these to your site. There are several sites that provide such services free. At **delphi.com** and **topica.com** it is easy to set up a message board, where site users can post messages and a chat room, which can be used for online 'conversations'. For example, you could invite a group of friends to an online chat to discuss a partic-ular subject, or to quiz an expert who remains online for an hour or two answering questions. Encourage visitors to make contributions and to use the message boards to post questions or to provide infor-mation.

Be aware of the email requests received and try to accommodate answers to those on your site. A page of **Frequently Asked Ques-tions (FAQs)** is useful if the site provides information. Produce a regular ezine or electronic magazine that has news about you and your site with plenty of snippets that may interest readers. Remember to throw in a few good jokes. Ezines can be a great marketing opportu-nity, so use them to advantage. Gain enough subscribers and you may be able to gain income from advertisers on your ezine. Again there are places that will maintain your mailing list for you. A good example of such a site is **listbot.com**.

Create links

Portal sites are commercially important, and many big companies are trying to cash in on this market. You can take advantage of their eagerness by using the links such sites provide. These links on your front page may enhance the site – but do make sure they are relevant. A constantly updated news ticker tape is available from http://www.7am.com/. It places a little Applet on your page and this ticker-tapes news across your screen. It is not obstructive and it provides some movement and useful information. With **multi-crawl.com** a search engine facility can be provided that displays, using your own site design. A search engine consisting of links that you and the visitors to your site provide can be created using **linkbank.net**. This also provides a daily check to ensure the links are still working, adding to the professionalism on the site.

Translations can be important. Not everyone in the world reads English and offering a translation of your work could be a help to sell those foreign rights. The site http://babelfish.altavista.com offers an online translation service; it is not perfect but it is free. Or www.transexp.com will allow a link, so that site visitors can quickly obtain a translation.

Dictionaries are clearly important to writers. Websters' site at http://www.m-w.com allows links to their sites, offering an opportunity for an extensive online resource.

Offer the owners of other sites a link on your pages. Choose relevant, even competing sites, asking them to create a link in return. These links should not be on the opening pages of your site as there is little point in sending a new visitor to your site away before they have had a chance to look at your material. The next generation of search engines will use the number of links *to* a site as an indicator of its popularity.

Finally, ask people to **'Please bookmark this site'**.

9

WEBSITE MAINTENANCE

A website is the window through which the rest of the world can see you. It offers great opportunities for individuals to reach out to a wide audience. The VDU screen that displays your work is the same size as that used to show the products of huge multi-national companies. To make it work requires careful and continuous maintenance.

One of the joys of running a website is that it is there all the time; whether you are having a bad hair day or not, your site will be ready with a cheery greeting and a happy smile to meet all your potential customers. It is also relatively cheap. No real office space is required. It is possible to work from an 'office' which is a back bedroom or the corner of a dining room. There are no printing and postage costs to direct mail copy to editors and publishers. Everything can be emailed, as most publishing companies are now on the internet. It is as necessary to the functioning of their businesses as the telephone, the fax machine and the photocopier. The internet is already becoming even more important. It enables writers to contact their customers using just a telephone, a computer, and a modem or network connection to your ISP (internet service provider).

Once a simple website is ready, a computer must be found that will ensure that it can be viewed 24 hours a day, 365 days a year. Choose a reliable internet service provider (ISP) for this task. (It is not really feasible to think of running your own server. It needs a powerful computer and some means of allowing thousands of people to access your site all the time.) An internet service provider will give you space on their computer for your website, ensuring that it can be viewed by thousands of people at the same time, all the time.

It is at this early stage that you need to make an important decision, one that may have long-term consequences. There is an explosion in the provision of free websites, making it very cheap and easy to build your own site. There are advantages to be had from such services; they are cheap and they will help you by providing sample pages that you can adapt for your own site.

Free websites

Such 'free' websites normally use your ISP's name, which means that the address (URL: Unique Reference Locator) for your site becomes something like http://www.service.provider.co.uk/~personalweb-pages/yourname/index.html. That is a bit of a mouthful and it does not look very professional but who cares? The writer wishing to look professional should think carefully before using such services because they do have some weaknesses.

For example, you may receive more email than you would like, from companies who have been given your email address by your ISP. But you should be able to stop that happening, as most ISPs care about their customers and will allow you to filter out unwanted emails. So it may not be a problem, but email spamming (sending copies of an email to hundreds of people that do not know who you are) can become a nuisance.

Your free site may be obliged to display advertisements chosen by your ISP. This is one way in which the ISP can attract that advertising, and so make a profit. Again, that may not be a serious concern, but if the website is to become an important promotional vehicle for your talents, then advertising someone else's products may not be much help.

Your chosen ISP could go bust. As the industry expands there will be some casualties, take-overs, mergers and changes. One result will be that all the links to your site could disappear. All those visitors who have bookmarked your site because they intend to return one day would also disappear if that happened. Once your site has gone it will be impossible to trace them; and when they try to connect to your site at some time in the future they will only find an error message on the screen.

You may decide to move to another, cheaper or nicer ISP (internet service provider). No real problems with that, you may think, but do not be fooled. Moving servers can also undo all your hard work. You may be able to tell your friends that you have moved, but once again you cannot tell your visitors, nor can you tell the many hundreds of webcrawlers that have indexed your site. All of those contacts will be lost when you move. It is like losing your address book.

Free space will only rarely allow the use of technical add-ons such as cgi, or electronic commerce, or email forwarding. It will not provide you with any information about the usage of your site, how many visitors, what pages on your site they looked at or where they came from. Such information can be invaluable.

Page counters

Once created a website attracts visitors. Page counters measure how many visitors you have. They are often provided by your ISP, and there are several sites that will allow links to page counters. Their use can be counter-productive. If there are only a few visitors, your site will look unattractive to others, who want to feel part of a crowd. Strange psychology, but true. If you use a page counter, it should be placed at the bottom of the page – well below the page displays – so that only the site webmaster (that's you) is likely to view it. An ISP which is dedicated to providing website space will provide detailed statistics, showing the number of visitors to the site, where they came from, the pages visited and the pages downloaded.

Search engines and crawlers

In the early days of the site many of your visitors will be automatic software programs whose job it is to speed around the web indexing all the pages they find. Once indexed your site will begin to appear on search engines, and perhaps 80% of your visitors will result from links from search engines. As the web is growing at such a phenomenal rate some search engines are overwhelmed with data. A search can reveal millions of links, and this overload of information is counter-productive. Search engines are constantly looking at the data they are collecting. One result is that many search engines and webcrawlers are no longer bothering to visit personal pages on free servers.

So you may want to pay

Choose a reliable ISP, one that you believe will last and stick with them. An ISP (internet service provider) is a company which has a computer or a bank of computers, which has large and fast connections to the rest of the internet. Hundreds of people at any one time can read your website pages, which are available 24 hours a day, every day of the year.

Most ISPs will sell you an email facility plus access to the internet as well as the webspace for your site. They may also give you some instructions showing you how to create your own site.

They may have sample pages, as templates, so that you can get started. Use these templates to give a standard style to the whole of your site, one that suits your own needs. It is not very difficult, particularly if you start simply and add new pages as they seem necessary. Word processing programs also allow pages to be created in HTML.

Buy your own domain name. It is likely that we will all have our own domains eventually, so why not now? Is your site just a joke or are you seriously trying to do business on the web? Having your own domain name gives stability. With **http://www.mydomain.co.uk** the website can be placed on any ISP's computer, anywhere in the world. You can move it around yet it will always remain a part of you. Your email address will always be the same, wherever you happen to be, and your website will always have that same reliable name. It can have mirror sites, allowing faster access from the other side of the world but it will still work when your first ISP breaks down. It looks more professional and will be indexed by the search engines.

The alternative is to use a website name allocated to you by your ISP. Then your website address will be **http://www.yourname.isp-name.co.uk** or **http://www.isp-name/~yourname/**

The major problem with having your own domain name is – it costs money. Not a fortune, but you must first buy the domain name licence, which is renewable every two years, and then pay the ISP that will host your domain. The name may cost £100–150, and hosting may cost another £250 or more per year. These charges vary, and they are falling as competition increases.

This may seem too high a price, but the choice must be made. Writers on the internet need to change the way they think of them-selves. This is a new medium, and you must understand something about the technology that makes the internet work to be able to exploit it properly. It is not that difficult. There are some strange new terms to confront, but the internet is full of helpful people. Be honest and they will try to understand and support you.

Your attitude must change from being a writer to becoming some-thing of an online publisher. You can cooperate with others to produce joint projects. The web is about linkages, and your work will also form links with others. Your website is the shop window for all this activity.

The WWW is growing very fast – doubling in size every 100 days – making it the fastest growing business there has ever been. And this is just the beginning, because the internet will link up with TV and radio, making it a remarkable communications network that will influence every part of all our lives. Being able to switch on the lighting in your home from your mobile phone as you drive home will be an example of this revolution. As digital broadcasting replaces analogue radio waves there is competition to dominate the communications industry; with set-top boxes on TVs allowing access to a wide range of services, including the internet. In time most business transactions will use digital communications.

It is important to ensure that the site is highly rated by search engines. This can become an obsession, with panic setting in because the site cannot be found on Yahoo, or Lycos or Excite. Search engines are constantly looking for new ways to improve the service they provide. It is not easy to keep up with the latest trends, and to try to do so may be a waste of energy. It is more productive to make sure that your site is well known within your own area of interest. Try searching for your own subject matter; note which categories are used by the search engines, and then submit your pages to the search engine using those categories. That will improve the chances of someone finding your page during a search.

Some sites now have their own search engines, providing links to other sites that cover the subject matter of the site. This can avoid trawling through huge amounts of irrelevant information. It is possible to personalise the information display, and **portal sites** are growing in importance as they allow the user to construct opening pages that display the news and information they require.

Making your site

Open up the **View: Source** box of your browser (it is **View: Page Source** in Netscape and the HTML coding used to create the page will be revealed. At the top of this page the opening section is called <HEAD>. Within this area the page <TITLE> and <METATAB CONTENT>'s lines are inserted. These do not appear on the browser screen but are accessible to programs such as webcrawlers.

There is usually a metatab called <AUTHOR> – put your own name in there as bold as brass <META CONTENT= "Trevor Lockwood & Karen Scott" NAME= "Author">.

Another is called <DESCRIPTION> – use this to put in a descriptive phrase that will tell readers what the page is all about. This phrase will often be collected by webcrawlers and will appear on search engines beside the link to your site. Take some care to make it succinct, informative and relevant because many people will decide whether to jump to your page as a result of that description.

<META CONTENT= "Writer's Guide to the Internet: clear and useful information for writers who want to use the internet" NAME= "Description">

Below that is the section called 'Keywords '. This is a list of all the words and short phrases that can be chosen to describe your site. It tries to match the words inserted into search engine query boxes. The page for this book at http://www.author.co.uk/writers-guide/ contains the following keywords: <META CONTENT= "electronic publishing, online publishing, write, writers, authors, publish, publishers, UK, England, writing, publishing, writers guide, internet publishing, internet writing, how-to, Allison & Busby, Karen Scott, Trevor Lockwood" NAME= "KeyWords">

The last and most important is the **Title** of the page. This entry appears along the top of browser page and is an important descriptive device. Some search engines will use this instead of the **Description tag.** It needs to be short (less than 25 words) and sweetly succinct: <TITLE>Writer's Guide to the Internet by Trevor Lockwood & Karen Scott, published by Allison & Busby, home page at author.co.uk</TITLE>

Make sure that all links and graphics on your page have a text alternative; many people surf the web with the graphics facility on their browser switched off. Then the space where the graphic would have been appears on screen as a blank square box. By including a text alternative those words will appear in the box. Also ensure that the dimensions of any graphic are included with the HTML of the page. If the graphic is just allowed to display, a small box will appear on screen while the picture is loading. If the dimensions are included, the opening box will be the right size. This ensures the text can be read clearly while the picture is still loading. It is surprising how few commercial sites bother to provide alternative explanations. (These are essential for the many blind people who use the internet, as their audio browsers will read the alternative text for them.)

The webcrawlers report back to their search engines and directories, who then file away the information obtained into their huge databases and as a result of a search, visitors come to your site. But not all search engines use crawlers. The biggest and most important engine **http://www.yahoo.com** uses another method. You have to submit details of the page to search directories like **Yahoo.** They will then either accept your submission automatically and include your pages in the parts of the index you suggest or they will visit your site to check it out first. In the case of **Yahoo** information is submitted by first going to the relevant index on their site, the place where you believe your site should be listed. Once there, click through to 'suggest a site' where four pages of information have to be completed. Make sure you submit to several different parts of the site; even though they ask for suggestions, the links do not always appear. They have directories for writers, for publishers and for hundreds of different subject areas. Consider these carefully and submit your site, or specific pages on your site, to the relevant indexes.

Some search engines demand money from companies who want to be in the top listing. A place in the top ten – the sites first displayed as a result of a query search – can be vital. Not everyone searching will move on down the list; there may be millions of references. That said, there will always be categories that cannot attract such blatant commercialism. As a writer you will probably be able to index your site within such areas and so avoid the competition of commercial sites.

Submit your site under your author name and any category that fits the genre of your work. Make sure that your publisher submits your name under their imprint. Consider submitting under regional guides, and to the host of sites that have connections with your work. The Arts Council (http://www.arts.org.uk) is one obvious place to start.

Submitting information about your website to search engines can be time consuming. There are companies that will automate that process for you. Their charges are quite low considering the time they save and the extra visitors that will come to your site as a result. Use a site such as **http://www.submit.com.** to send information to over 400 search engines.

Search engines are important and you must ensure that you have submitted your site to all the major engines. Do not get obsessed with them or you will be spending too much time getting a good rating on a search engine at the expense of writing.

Establishing a reputation on the internet takes time. People are naturally cautious and building personal links is vitally important. Word of mouth (or email), as with other forms of advertising, is usually the most effective.

Email the owners of pertinent sites asking that they create a link to your site, always offering to reciprocate. Establishing a set of useful links can attract visitors to your site, as good contacts are useful and will encourage visitors to the site. It is important that those links are checked regularly, as your reputation will suffer if too many of the links you provide do not work. Services such as **http://www.linkbank.com** offer a site search engine facility. They will check your links every day, putting aside stale links so that you can check whether they still exist. For a small outlay such a facility improves the image of the site and increases credibility.

Having your own website is just the opening statement. It is merely a shop window down a back street unless visitors are persuaded to the site. Maintaining the site is vital if interest is to be retained and visitors are to return. There is no completely reliable formula but several points must be kept in mind:

Make sure the site works

Check that all the links go to the page they are supposed to reach, and that the page actually exists. There are companies that will check the links on your site. One very useful site is http:///www.netmechanic.com and this will provide different versions of your graphics, frequently making them smaller in file size and thus faster to download. Avoid the over-use of graphics and make sure they work quickly. To display a picture on the web you will not need more than 72 dpi (dots per inch). The high resolution demanded by normal printing methods is not necessary.

Design for the user

Writing for the web requires consideration of both form and content. Authors should think about writing directly in HTML (or at least with HTML-compatible style sheets), previewing screens as they write and working with the page designer on the multimedia elements. You need to know what it will look like on the screen as you write.

The copy should be tightly structured, and that structure should be immediately apparent to the reader.

Try to use the same graphic images on all your pages, introducing one or two new elements to each page. Browsers retain the pages visited in temporary file folders on the user computer. Once an image has been downloaded during a visit to your site it can be quickly reloaded to the screen from the user's own computer, and this is obviously much faster than the internet link.

Retain interest

Change the site frequently. Some programs will allow global replacement of items such as background page colour. Move pages around, redesign them, and include more and more content. Material need not be discarded. Most websites allow at least 5 Mb of space, which gives oodles of room to archive old text material. Keep it on the site, just reduce its importance by cutting down the number of links to that page, or by deliberately stating that it can now be found in an archive section.

If files are too large, allow them to be downloaded as zip files, as MS Word document files, or as ftp files. Encourage visitors to download such material, telling them to open it in their word processors or to print it on paper.

Include links to other sites. Take care to link only to those sites that you believe will interest your site visitors and make sure the links always work.

Try email lists, or an ezine

Email is the most powerful force on the internet. A website may display everything beautifully but it is not much better than that scarecrow in a field if visitors do not arrive. Cherish your email contacts, save their email addresses (I like to call them eddresses), and send them an occasional email to keep them aware of and interested in your activities.

The personal approach is always best. As writers we are not in the numbers game, we are not intent on persuading the whole wide world to drink our particular version of sugary fizz. Our contacts should become our friends and they deserve to be treated as such from the start. Email messages should always be sent individually. Even if you want to send the same message to a number of people it is worthwhile to cut and paste the same message into a personal message for every contact rather than lumping them all together.

As emails are received, send a reply as soon as practicable, then place both the message and the reply in a folder. Some time later send another note. A simple 'How are you getting on?' can work wonders.

You may decide to contact your growing list of internet friends by writing an ezine (an electronic magazine) that is sent out to subscribers. Sites such as http://www.listbot.com allow you to set up a whole range of facilities, including mailing lists. An invitation is sent to anyone who may be interested (and Listbot will do this for you), inviting them to subscribe to the list. The recipient can unsubscribe at any time just by sending an email. The choice is theirs; it is much better than spamming (sending unsolicited emails) into the unknown. This can alienate people forever.

Your ezine can include anything. Think of it as a magazine or a newsletter. Add variety and interest, and keep it short. If you use

Listbot this will happen anyway, as they may restrict the size of your mailing.

Most ezines are sent as plain text, but you could consider using an HTML version, which would allow for the inclusion of graphics and the page layout found on web pages. But using HTML will increase the overall file size and may not be available to everyone, and it may mean that a commercial mailing list program such as Lyris (http://www.lyris.com) would have to be purchased.

Have a good jokes section or an interest area

One of the most successful pages created on the author.co.uk site was called; 'Chocolate is better than Sex'. It was just a light-hearted, and hardly risqué, list of chocolate's attributes. It attracted loads of visitors because those two words are often searched for on the internet. Put together, they increased the 'hit' rate exponentially.

Most of the visitors to that page were not interested in the rest of the site but some of them were, and included on the page was a short snappy description, and a link, to the rest of the pages. That page brought an increase in the number of visitors to the other parts of the site.

That is an extreme example, but it does show that interest can be created in different ways, and that we all like to relax sometimes. The site also included a crossword, with the clues linked to an article about the history of swimming pools, which the puzzler was encouraged to read first. This is a useful trick, as it reinforces the learning process, and to do is to remember. Consider using options that will interest visitors to the site: word searches or opportunities to send emails to a chat room, a guest sign-in page, or a catalogue of interesting books. You may have a diary of forthcoming events, certainly plenty of jokes, even a short biography with your photograph or free material that can be downloaded – perhaps a collection of your own work or a short bibliography; all this can add interest to your pages, making visitors return.

With links from these pages of general interest back to your own work you can encourage browsers to come back. These pages must be designed with users in mind. What do they want? Look at the statistics provided by your ISP, which show the movements of visitors to your site. Where do they go, how long do they stay? Try to fathom out what they really want from your site.

Create links to other sites and check those links

Whatever magic the search engines can create by attracting visitors it is very important to maintain and encourage links within your own circle of interest. We all live in small worlds, surviving as the result of contacts we make with a relatively small number of people. We must keep in touch with these people. Search out other sites like your own, or ones that may be interested in your work. If you have an article or book published then ensure the publisher creates a link from their site to your own. Links are important. Email the site owner, tell them why they should create a link to your site, tell them you will reciprocate – perhaps even by hosting a copy of their opening page on your site, making the link look seamless.

Encourage feedback

Creating a website is like all writing. It is a lonely business that does little more than encourage uncertainty. Does the world really like what is on your site? Are you really doing some good, or just wasting your time? The only objective way to find this out are by asking and listening. The questions need not be blatant, although the direct approach is often the best. Put a guest sign-in page on your site; encourage people to leave their email address and to comment upon what they have seen. Read the emails you receive very carefully; often they will tell you about broken links, or your failure to do something properly, or they may ask questions which are not answered on your site.

Take note of what is said, and adapt accordingly. Give visitors what they want. Your site, as a professional writer, is not about self-aggrandisement, it is the most valuable advertising medium you will ever have for your work.

Advertise your URL

'Advertise' often means paying for promotion. We take adverts in papers, airtime on radio stations, direct mail copy to hundreds. Such advertising costs money. Conventional advertising agencies are now trying to promote the same principles on the web. They may succeed for big business but such methods are not useful to writers. 'Advertise' by drawing attention to the services you can provide. Make sure that all your emails contain a signature (a short piece of text that is automatically inserted into every email message). The signature must have your email and website addresses clearly shown, together with a brief line of text that explains who you are, and what you do. Do the same on all your snail-mail letterheads. Try to include a reference to your services, and to your website, in all the articles you write. Push your URL in the face of all you see! When asked for information, refer enquirers to your website. The site can provide detailed material information about your work.

Paying for adverts on the internet is unlikely to bring any worthwhile return. There are better ways. One writer submitted an article about proofreading to a free ezine, which was sent daily to several thousand webmasters. He was offered a contract to proofread 76 in-house journals for a multinational company as a result. Life can take some strange turns, so be flexible and ready to meet the new challenges as they arise.

Consider banners

A banner advert can often be seen on sites. It is usually a rectangular box at the top of the page through which to click to another site.

Consider placing banner adverts on your site very carefully indeed and be sceptical. Why should you receive a visitor to your site, then have them immediately click away somewhere else? Do you gain anything from that, in money or credibility, fame or fortune? Is that hard-won visitor ever likely to return?

You will often see banner advertisements in the middle of an opening page on a site. Many search engines carry banner ads, as they are undoubtedly gaining income based on the 'click-through' rate to the advertiser.

As a writer you are unlikely to attract enough visitors to your site to encourage a banner ad supplier to pay you for the service. Or, if they do, the amount you receive will be insignificant compared with the loss you suffer.

But some banner ads can be worthwhile. There are groups that link together; one small group is for writer/publishers at http://www.austensharp.com/webring.htm which members place on their own pages, allowing click-throughs to other members' sites. These links change every time the page is opened, producing variety for your visitor. Even so they are best confined to the more obscure pages on your own site. Make sure that visitors have a look at several pages on your own site before presenting them with a banner ad to another site.

The internet is not just an interface, allowing us to copy files, launch programs, to communicate quickly and easily; it is also an art form, a window through which we shall come to view history and much of our current culture. At this stage in its development there is too much emphasis upon graphics and display. That will change; content must become the dominant theme if the web is to survive. Writers will become the major contributors to the internet, although they may continue to appear subordinate – as they are in film and TV – with other players in the team usually taking the plaudits. As writers we are used to the directors, actors and other bit-players taking the bows. Yet they all rely upon our words, our initiating genius. The internet will not change that fact. It will provide untold new opportunities.

10

ONLINE PUBLISHERS

Publishers and agents

Publishers and agents are believed to trawl the internet looking for writers, and some sites are well known for showcasing the best fiction on the internet (try **Pif** http://www.pifmagazine.com). Getting your work on sites like this may be worthwhile if your quest is to be noticed. However, going straight to the top may prove to be even more successful. Many online publishers do accept email submissions and are happy to look at your work. However, the fact that a publisher has a website doesn't necessarily mean that they accept email submissions as a matter of course.

Submission procedures

Submission procedures will vary from publisher to publisher, whether online or not, but there are several points to bear in mind:

- The safest way to ensure that you send your manuscript in the right format and to the right person is to make a general enquiry by email before you send it.
- Secure a specific name within an editorial department.
- Find out if the publisher will accept documents as attachments to an email or would rather receive the synopsis and sample chapters embedded in the text of the email.
- Don't send a manuscript to an online publisher without first making sure that they are willing to accept it; this point cannot be overemphasized.

Below is a short list of publishers who have websites – there are many more out there – these are just a few of the better-known names.

Allison & Busby
http://www.allisonandbusby.ltd.uk
Amherst Media Books
http://members.aol.com/photobook/

Bantam Doubleday Dell
http://www.bdd.com/
Bloomsbury
http://www.bloomsbury.co.uk
Coach House Books
http://www.chbooks.com
Hodder & Stoughton
http://www.u-net.com/hodder/
Loki Books
http://www.lokibooks.u-net
Macmillan Publishers Ltd
http://www.macmillan.co.uk
Penguin
http://www.penguin.co.uk/
Pulp Books
http://www.pulpfact.demon.co.uk
Random House
http://www.randomhouse.com/
Secker & Warburg
http://www.reedbooks.co.uk/
Simon & Schuster
http://www.simonsays.com

A brief interlude – 'e' or not

It is necessary at this juncture to clarify the types of publishers to be found on the internet.

- Print-based publishers use websites to promote themselves, the writers they publish and the books they want to sell. They don't publish or sell any writer's material on that website; it is simply another promotional tool.
- E-publishers also have websites but they use their sites to offer for sale the work of the writers they are trying to promote. Anyone can download the work of an author listed on the website for a cost similar to the price of a paperback or a hardback or less, or on a pay-to-view basis. The writer is usually paid a percentage of this in royalties.
- The only difference between a traditional publisher and an electronic publisher is that the product is in electronic form, rather than on paper.

When is a book not a book?

Apparently when it's an e-book is probably the likeliest answer. An electronic book is a book saved as a computer file; it is then offered for sale as a download from the publisher's website to your computer or on a disk. However, there are many references on the internet to e-books being an electronic form of a print book. There are some early examples of small hand-held PCs (such as Softbook) which enable a user to read the e-book in much the same way as a normal book, although in an electronic format. (These will be referred to in more detail later.) References to e-books on the internet take in both these definitions and this can be confusing. There are also many discussions on and off the internet that take in these different definitions and run wild with them. No doubt you will come across many of them; it really is up to you whether you choose to engage directly in these discussions or read them purely to keep up to date with developments in this area.

How the online publisher makes money

Online publishers make money in a variety of ways, but the three most common are:

- Advertising revenue
- Timed subscriptions
- Pay-per-view

Advertising revenue is usually generated by banner ads in one of three ways: exposure, by click, or by action. *Pay by exposure* means that each time a banner ad is displayed, the publisher receives a credit for a percentage of a cent or penny. *Pay by click* means that each time the user clicks on the advertisement and is taken to the advertiser's website, the publisher receives credit for a few cents or pence. *Pay by action* means that the publisher is given a credit for each user who actually buys the product advertised in the ad. **Amazon.co.uk** works in this way; if you link your site to theirs you will receive a percentage of every sale made from that link. Many commercial websites use one if not more of these methods to earn revenue.

The user reading the free portion of the material on a website and then giving credit card details for a subscription usually starts a timed subscription. The publisher's computer program will establish a user name and password, allowing the user access to the site for a fixed period of time. Automatic renewal is often an option on these sites and the subscription is taken from the original credit card details.

Pay-per-view publishers require the user to pay for each item of text downloaded. 1st Books (http://www.1stbooks.com) works in this way.

How the writer is paid
One of the primary concerns of the author who writes specifically for the internet is the royalties paid for work published on these online publishing websites, and what percentage of these royalties the author should look to receive. This could be based on (a) the time the work is made available on the site, (b) the number of readers allowed to see the work before the publisher owes more money to the author, or (c) a percentage of the cost of downloading the work from the publisher's site. These terms need to be set out clearly and it really is in everyone's interest for there to be a written signed contract detailing terms. This would be similar to the standard contract that exists between publisher and author in the print-based publishing industry.

Online media links

Omnimedia Electronic Publishing
Omnimedia is in the process of compiling the most comprehensive list of internet sites that offer electronic books or electronic publishing information. Presently, they have over 70 links.
http://www.awa.com/library/omnimedia/links.html

Northern Lights Internet Solutions
This site lists hundreds of publishers from at least 30 countries. Many on the list are speciality publishers, and predominantly market and sell paper books. It doesn't tell you, however, which internet sites deal in electronic books.
http://www.lights.com/publisher/

World Publishing-Industry
Links to many sites to do with publishing online, and writing and publishing in general, a good search facility.
http://publishing-industry.net/

Mainstream Publishers
Good links to writing-related issues including online publishing.
http://writerexchange.miningco.com/MSUB13.HTM

Songs Online – Music Publishing/Publishers
Promotes songs, songwriters, songwriting and music publishers by

showcasing their songs/music in RealAudio. Music professionals can find new song/song-writing material for their upcoming projects.
http://www.songsonline.com/

ForeWord Online

The complete internet resource for independent publishers and booksellers. Foreword Magazine is devoted to independent publishers, university press and independent booksellers.
http://forewordmagazine.com/

Ravensyard

A storytelling community for readers, writers, editors and publishers. Ravensyard Publishing Ltd., a publishing venture, sponsors this site which uses the internet to create the markets necessary to bring out new titles – on demand – of small-market books unavailable through traditional means.
http://ravensyard.com/

Mercury Publishing

Mercury Publishing Online Bookstore. Includes metaphysical, Celtic and mythology books. Quality books about spirituality, Celtic traditions and metaphysical arts.
http://www.mercurypublishing.com/

As Written

(Online) electronic showcase of unpublished literary works. Takes no responsibility for content. The author is responsible for fulfilling an order and money is then paid directly to them by As Written.
http://www.boldy1.demon.co.uk/

Australian Publishers Online

Australian Publishers Online Reed Books
http://www.reedbooks.com.au/
Butterworths
http://www.butterworths.com.au/
The Law Book Company
http://www.lbc.com.au

HyperBooks Online Bookstore

Hyperbooks is trying to create an online bookstore, selling electronic texts, software, games, or just about anything else that can be transmitted through the internet. They are committed to carrying a

wide variety of merchandise, and offer as easy and convenient a shopping experience as possible. Check out submission guidelines.
http://hyperbooks.com/

The Handbook for Ezine Publishers!
The first stop for ezine publishers. Tips, training and an ezine search engine.
http://ezinez.com/

Sharing Time Books Consortium
A new online catalogue for writers and publishers. The consortium is dedicated to promoting, marketing and providing a new online catalogue platform for booksellers, writers and publishers.
http://www.sharingtimebooks.com/

The World Wide Web Virtual Library
Lists of online publishers.
http://www.comlab.ox.ac.uk/archive/publishers.html

Publishers' Catalogues Home Page
Search for a publisher.
http://www.lights.com/publisher/

Open Book Systems (OBS)
A large book publisher with an extensive site available in four languages.
http://www.obs-us.com/obs/english/top.htm

The WWW VL Electronic Journals List
This is the WWW Virtual Library list of publishing companies which maintain World Wide Web or other internet resources.
http://www.edoc.com/

Editor & Publisher
Search newspaper listings by publication or country.
http://www.mediainfo.com/ephome/npaper/nphtm/online.htm

ASCAP
The American Society of Composers, Authors and Publishers. Events, membership info, links to resources in the music business, and a searchable database of performed music in the ASCAP repertory.
http://www.ascap.com/

Six of the best – e-book publishers online

When the first online book was nominated for the Booker Prize the print-based publishing industry's collective heart must have sunk. No one believed that it would happen so soon or even that it would happen at all. But it did happen and it has done more for the credibility of the e-book than any other single event. It has proved that work published on the internet can be of an equally high standard to that chosen by a traditional publisher; and has proved that e-publishers are just as rigorous in their choices as traditional publishers are.

Much has changed since the first online publishers' websites began to appear on the internet. Some of the early ones have gone and some of those that have stood the test of time do not appear to have changed very much. But those that have survived have grabbed the initiative and moved on. The changes are manifold; many of the 'old' online publishers used to charge authors to put their material on the website, now publishers are offering the author payment in the form of royalties.

There are still some e-publishers that are similar to print-based vanity publishers. They will take any old manuscript, put it on their website and charge the author. It is difficult to find out whether any of these authors make money but it is doubtful.

At the present time there are many good online publishers to be found on the internet and there is no need to risk your money. If your work is of a good standard and the e-publisher thinks your manuscript will be a success then you and he could make some money. That is how it should be. Try some of the e-publishers listed below.

OverDrive Press
As they say, 'BookWorks represents the future of digital publishing that will take your content to new destinations. It provides a wide spectrum of options for your publishing needs.' They require no money to be contributed by the author. Royalties are calculated as a percentage of net revenues. Take a look at their bookstore.
http://www.overdrive.com

BookAisle
They offer a variety of download and purchase options; they even have an associates' programme.
http://wwwbookaisle.com

PreviewBooks (Oak Tree Publishing)
A good site, which allows readers access to the first half of a book, and if they like what they see they can pay a fee to download the remainder. According to the publishing agreement, royalties are calculated on the number of 'remainders' sold.
http://www.preview.books.com

BiblioBytes
This site offers a number of 'free books' to download. It has a tendency to accept any new work, as long as it is properly formatted. The publication agreement offers authors a 35% royalty if any books are actually sold.
http://www.bb.com

Online Originals
This website is the home of the Booker Prize nominated e-book, *The Angels of Russia* by Patricia le Roy, an English novelist. It is also the home of a number of other online titles that have received good reviews in *The Times Literary Supplement*. They also offer the unique ability to receive the file in a format readable by 3Com's Palm Pilot, making the concept of the e-books into truly portable commodity. One title a month is offered for free download. Check out the site for their editorial policy.
http://www.onlineoriginals.com/

1st Books
Another large e-publisher. However, it only publishes books for free if they have been published before; unpublished authors can pay up to $500. The author, however, does receive the full profit on the book until their costs are recovered, and then a 40% royalty.
http://www.1st.books.com/

Hard Shell Word Factory
http://www.hardshell.com
Hard Shell Word Factory is a royalty-paying publisher of works for sale in electronic format from their site as downloads or disks-in-the-mail, as well as mail order. They don't offer advances, but their royalties (paid quarterly) are much higher than those offered by traditional publishers. Your work is made available for a full year with an option for renewal.

The realities of e-publishing

As any writer knows, traditional markets are becoming smaller and harder to crack. Publishers stay with the tried and tested best-selling authors and this leaves little room for the untried and untested first time author. But the electronic market is another matter; it is wide open and full of opportunities for the untried and untested as well as the tried and tested. In many cases the electronic publishing industry will take on work that breaks all the rules. Authors who have had success with other work but cannot get a work published because it breaks all the rules do seek publication on the internet because they know that they may succeed with a work that the print-based publishing industry wouldn't take on. But there are many other reasons for writers to move into the electronic market.

The advantages of e-publishing

- It takes less time for an electronic publisher to decide whether they want your book, and this means that you have more opportunities to present your work.
- There are no restrictions on word-count, no unnecessary editing to meet the word-count or padding out to meet the word-count.
- Plot and character restrictions do not exist.
- Most writers feel they have more control with an e-publisher. You can write what goes on the cover, or even design it yourself.
- The shelf life of e-books is greatly extended and writers often have the option to renew. This increases the chance of sales and income.
- Editors seem to be more accessible in electronic publishing. Most are only an e-mail away.
- Contracts issued by e-publishers are less complicated than those issued by traditional publishers.
- Publishing on the internet is just as legitimate as publishing in print.
- If you have a best-selling e-book your chances of getting into 'print' are greatly increased. Nothing sparks publisher interest more than the sound of a cash register.
- E-publishers don't pay advances to their writers, but they do pay much better royalties on the whole. These are usually in the region of 25–40% from every book you sell. Compared with the 10% given by print publishers this seems rather good.

The disadvantages of e-publishing

- One major disadvantage of being electronically published is the lack of respect. The general population is very wary of electronic publishing. It is still a baby in comparison to the print-based publishing industry and it will take time for it to achieve the high status of the traditional print medium. The impression is that if your book cannot be found in a local bookshop – and held up for the relatives to admire – it does not count.
- Some societies, organizations and writers' circles still do not welcome e-authors with open arms.
- The audience is still small and the percentage of the population that has access to the internet is limited. Public awareness is narrow.
- Reading e-books is quite difficult, but hand-held readers are becoming available to enable users to read electronic books. But they are expensive.
- Copyright is a big issue. A traditional publisher won't buy a book if they can't have first rights to it.

General guidelines and advice

- Do your own research if you are unsure if e-publishing is for you. Take a good look at some e-publishers' websites; read the material that is available.
- Don't sell to vanity e-publishers. These exist in much the same format on the internet as they do in the traditional publishing industry.
- Make sure you check out the credentials of any e-publisher you are considering. Try the Epic website for help at http://www.geocities.com/Paris/Metro/3900/. They provide a list of legitimate e-publishers.
- Having a website gives you a huge advantage. There are many free providers on the internet, including Angelfire at http://www.Angelfire.com and Tripod at http://www.Tripod.com.
- The internet has a vast array of communication, marketing and promotional tools available to writers. These include email, book-shops, newsgroups, bulletin boards, chat rooms and much more. Take advantage of them.
- Finally, even if you are determined to see your book in print, the internet really is too good an opportunity to miss. Neglecting it may be detrimental to your career.

Revolution or mutiny?

The World Wide Web has provided an instant distribution service for the writer. It is possible to write, edit, design and publish material on the internet and anyone can have access to it. But although this revolution has helped the writer there is still a tendency for the outside world to harp constantly on about quality . If anyone can have their work published on the internet, then where is the editorial control? Writers who do publish work on the internet, in whatever genre, only have to respond that e-publishers and editors of ezines are not charities; they are on the internet to make money and if editorial content is what attracts readers to their sites then quality, is of the utmost importance.

There is a vast difference between creating a website on which to put your work and having your book accepted by an e-publisher who offers royalties or having your article accepted by the editor of an ezine who pays for copy. These differences are very clear; but having your own website does provide a platform that enables you to have a presence on the internet. Every writer on the internet can make the distinction between personal websites and e-published work as can every e-publisher, editor and any other person connected with the writing industry. So why should e-publishing have a bad name?

The answer to the last question is not easy. Perhaps it can be put down to fear – fear of change, fear of the new, or even fear of technology. For the print-based publishing industry it means that their grip on the market is being loosened daily; for the writer it means accepting and taking on new challenges. For some writers this is a welcome change, for others it is an unacceptable risk: rather than dip their toes in the water they prefer to turn away from it.

Instead of dismissing the internet out of hand however, they would be well advised to see the new medium for what it is and to make room for it. Because whatever they may think, e-publishing and e-authors and the internet are here to stay.

11

PUBLISHING YOUR NOVEL ONLINE

Publishing your work online is rapidly developing into a significant publishing format. It offers several advantages when compared with conventional publishing methods. It is simple, making it relatively easy for anyone to produce an acceptable product once some simple skills are acquired. It is fast; write this morning, publish after lunch! There is no need to wait in the queues which form to see managing editors, graphic designers and printers. It is cheap; initial costs are low, assuming that you have a computer and some suitable word-processing software. It is adaptable and can be quickly altered as required, making it particular suitable for database publishing, where lists of names and addresses are to be published. Uniquely, it is inter-active, allowing the reader to respond to the original work. It also requires very few resources; having no need for paper, ink, or phys-ical transport or warehouse storage.

Smearing ink on dead trees is not dead. The internet is not going to replace the book. It is offering alternatives and the writer needs to consider how online publishing can be used to his or her advantage. The writer must adapt to the demands of the system. Writing for the net requires new skills. Most writers have moved from scratching a wet quill on paper and now use a word-processing program on a computer. A few years ago desktop publishing was a popular idea, but it required additional computer software and graphic design skills. Now, word-processing makes us all much more aware of the need to consider page layouts and we select suitable fonts with relative ease, allowing our machines to handle kerning, and other technical details, with ease. Most programs offer a range of templates that can be used if the process of page design becomes too tedious.

Writing for the internet does require new skills but our computers have already anticipated many of the demands. Most documents can be saved in the language of the World Wide Web, as HTML files. With most word processors all of the laborious programming goes on in the background, leaving the writer free to play with words.

The internet does require a new approach to the craft of writing. The VDU screen page is not just another page in a book. To call it a page is a misnomer as it has little in common with the page of a book. It is a different shape, and it can be modified by the reader, who is free to change the fonts and graphics you have carefully chosen for the screen page. A web page has links to other pages, enabling the reader (viewer, surfer or user) to flick quickly from one page to another. There is no linear progression. The story need not move sequentially or logically from one event to another.

That said, the internet could be used to display conventional novels, short stories, poems, plays or any other text. The website can be constructed so that the reader is taken from page 1 to page 2 and so on. The material can be displayed in HTML, allowing it to be read from the screen. Illustrations can be incorporated so that the entire book will look just like a conventional book, the only difference being that it is displayed on a VDU screen.

That is just the starting point for electronic publishing and is not really satisfactory. The electronic book is not easy to read from a VDU screen. The image can tire the eyes, and the VDU monitor squashes the pillow when you are trying to read from it in bed. It lacks the comfortable feel of a book.

Physical changes

Attempts are being made to overcome the difficulties in reading electronic text. Companies are developing new screen fonts that display crisp sharp images on screen and hand-held devices, so that you can snuggle underneath the duvet and read in bed. The first versions of these devices are expensive. Softbook from SoftBook Press and the RocketBook from NuovoMedia are flat tablets that you hold and read, just like a book. A simple rocker switch allows movements forward or backward one page, without scrolling. Using a stylus on the touch-sensitive screen enables you to leave bookmarks and to make notes in the margins. Each device holds a library of books. You can select the book you want and choose settings to adjusting the type size and brightness. You can also download new books.

Softbook is targeting the scientific and technical market, offering a replacement for heavy tomes containing information that changes frequently. RocketBook is attacking the mass-market paperback audience with cheaper (but not cheap) products.

These devices will become cheaper, and other hand-held computers – such as those made by **Psion**™ – will adapt to being used as text readers. An electronic version of the book is slowly evolving. It will probably look and feel something like a paper book but will present a flat screen that is designed to display text clearly.

These experiments may fail, but there is some certainty that an easily transportable device similar to a mobile phone will soon be developed. It will have innumerable applications; bringing together our need to access information with a range of communications systems. Why buy a newspaper every day, why waste trees and energy on books, just because we are tied into a paper-based delivery system? That will change. The newspapers and books will not disappear, but they will be presented in a different form. The day is not far off when one small machine will accommodate a laptop computer, a PDA, a cell phone, a pager, an audio CD player, and an electronic book.

There is a long way to go and many obstacles to overcome. The paper book lasts a lifetime; the electronic e-book has a battery life of hours; the paper book is of fixed length and cannot be changed, but it is durable and can display illustrations perfectly. The e-book doesn't weigh very much and can update its content quickly from the internet. Pictures are not very well displayed at present but the quality will improve.

Electronic publishing may require new display devices. Certainly the physical world of computing is about to change. We can speculate whether access to the internet will be made easier by a TV set or a chip implant into our brains, or by flat-screen displays that replace the wallpaper in our homes and offices. The writer needs to be aware of these developments. They will provide grist to his mill.

Writing approaches

Let us say it again: writing for the web requires a new approach. The VDU screen presents a small target. The opening page needs to describe the contents of the rest of the work clearly and succinctly. Perhaps it can provide a road map of the narrative which can be used to click forward and backwards through the text. Readers value interactivity and will follow a story if they feel rewarded and in control.

Web users tend to scan the page, picking up visual clues. This is not reading but it is processing information. The human brain is very good at picking up clues from a variety of sources and assessing their value. It is an instinctive process unlike reading, which must be taught. Web pages need to contain instant visual clues that indicate what the page is all about, and where it will lead the user. In a conventional book format one of the opening pages would be a contents page. An electronic contents page will contain much more than one found in a book. It will certainly contain the author's biographical details, with links to other pages where detailed information can be found, links to the publisher's website, or to other books they have written, or to books of a similar genre. Those links may not be blocks of text. They can be pictures, cartoons, video links or even verbal instructions.

Within the text and on the website it is possible to include links that are no more than short diversions; perhaps to display a map, to give a more detailed historical footnote, or perhaps to provide a fuller description. This is like looking up a note at the back of a book, but the link access is quicker and easier. The thread of the story is not lost, the narrative is continued but the reader can choose whether to read the detail or not. In paper books the author must decide what is to be included from the mass of background material that has been collected in preparing the work. The electronic text, one that is following the linear progression of the paper book, can include links to any amount of material that may be extraneous to the plot but which add colour and detail to the narrative. The reader can choose which of many pathways they wish to follow.

Major exterior hypertext links, those that move outside the website or link to other works, should be clearly marked, for example in a list or in a short paragraph. Within a complete work these links require careful consideration. External links can easily be broken, or disappear altogether, and so diminish the quality of your work. Do you really want someone to leave your site and move to another in the middle of a story?

If there is a large amount of text, prompt the reader to print it out. There's no shame in printing, and a complex set of specifications or a densely written narrative is more easily read from paper than from screen displays. This combination of forms, electronic display combined with printing to read off-screen, allows for interesting works. Imagine an on-screen story, with an opening display that briefly outlines the story, a taster of what is to come (like the blurb found on the back of a book). The reader is left to make the choice: to read a shortened version on screen or to download to print a longer, more detailed version. Such choices can be offered anywhere within the narrative.

If a page is to be downloaded the print format should be properly considered. The **Adobe**™ **Acrobat** reader is freely available and enables any **.pdf** file to be printed in exactly the way it was intended to look. Acrobat is fast replacing **PostScript**™ as the transfer medium of choice between publishers and printers.

The reader is in a partnership with the writer on the web. Due attention must be given to the voice and tone of the writing and the web writer must always consider the physical actions of the reader;

clicking, scrolling and posting within the creation process. It helps to write material for the web in HTML format, checking how the work will display on a browser as you progress.

Remember that hypertext links are choices made by the author or page designer; they will not always match the needs of the reader. Be critical at all times as you create links. The author exercises considerable control over the pathways the reader will follow.

While the reader plays an active part as they chart a course through the work they are following determined routes, structured by the author. This compound approach is initially difficult to conceive. We are used to reading from the start of a story, progressing through the middle and coming to the end. Online publishing need not use that progression. There is a network of paths, offering the reader a continual choice.

Links
Every page can contain links to the contents page, to a bibliography or an index, to footnotes, as well as the main text of the piece. It can also provide much more, with graphics, animations, video and audio together with links to a CD-ROM or even to other websites.

These links are unlike those of a learned work, where references are intended to be examined and are often used to support the argument of the text. With hypertext links there is not necessarily any veracity or even any agreed association between the content of the page and the linked page. That kind of rigour has not yet arrived on the internet. Both writer and reader are warned. Truth is not always a viable concept on the internet.

Hypertext links allow jumps between concepts while also allowing exploration of related information. There need not be a conceivable end. Indeed there are those who hope that the web will eventually contain the sum total of all human knowledge. This idea can lead to a loss of discipline; the vast potential of the content mixes together with the strange technologies of the internet to overwhelm the writer.

Digital literacy is about content that is interactive. Too many sites still remain mere copies of the world of print. Several new problem-solving skills are required to succeed with using online resources and there is a greater need to evaluate everything the internet displays. You may not believe everything you read in the newspapers now but at least editors and journalists exercise considerable evaluation on your behalf. They run the risk of being sued or losing their reputations if they do not rigorously test their sources. Material on the web is different. Anyone can put it there, and they may not be telling the truth!

The copyright of electronic work is still a minefield. Many book and broadcasting contracts are for the duration of copyright. Electronic publishing is changing rapidly, and new developments could quickly overtake existing contractual arrangements. It is wise to limit the licence to a specified number of years: two to five years for straight text reproduction, perhaps three to six years where the work involves customised software or a multimedia development where the electronic publisher is making a large capital investment in the product. Organisations such as the **Authors Licensing & Copyright Society** are involved in protecting authors' rights in this area and can provide good advice to their members.

Composite works abound on the web, with many authors involved in a project. Often royalties are divided pro rata between all those whose work is included. This may be logical where a royalty is being divided between a number of similar contributors (e.g. five novelists). But it is not easy to define a pro rata contribution when dealing with different forms of material. Text takes up much less disk space than pictures or music, and other types of contributor (e.g. artists, composers or the software programmer) may also receive a royalty. The size of each individual's rising royalty should be clearly stated. If that is not possible when the initial contract is drawn up – which is frequently the case – the size of the royalty should be left for agreement when more is known about the creative input.

Authors may settle for a fee if their contribution is small, but then it should be paid on delivery rather than on publication, and should be based on the material requested and delivered rather than on the amount used in the finished product. It may be possible to agree that further fees should be payable in specified circumstances. Ensure that proper advice is obtained before signing any contract.

The internet is not a passive activity; it is not like television, where you can just allow yourself to be subsumed by garbage, or even like a book where the arguments presented have been carefully constructed by the author and subjected to editorial control. Critical thinking is required when using the internet. It is not the same as any other medium. There has been a paradigm shift, for the internet is not subject to any real form of central control, certainly not of content, although we must all abide by its technical protocols. To use the web requires intelligence, something we all possess to a greater or lesser degree.

It is important to realise that the web writer is not addressing a mass audience; even though millions of people have access to the internet, each of them comes through their own individual channel. And it is a channel over which they have absolute control. This is a democratic process, at least for now.

It is an exciting prospect. For some time it has been suggested that linking computers together into a network would double the performance and value of each computer. What does that mean for the internet? The human brain contains 10,000 million cells, combined together to make something very special, with added value. What will happen as the internet gives us all the capacity to link together? Will we create a super-human?

Finding out who is responsible for the material on the internet can be difficult. If you want to include the work of other writers for more than a brief extract, then permission must be obtained. Look for an eddress (email or website). It can tell you a lot, and be used to put you in touch with the author or publisher. A polite note, composed while you are offline, and sent to the author, will often produce results. If you are really stuck look at the 'Document: Information' screens. At least it will tell you where the page is lodged.

It is not too difficult to see how a conventional book can be transposed to the web, and how the linkages provided by HTML, and the ability to add colour, audio and even video can be used to improve upon the standard linear format of a book printed on paper. Remember that the word 'novel' originally meant something 'new, fresh, young'. The internet offers the creative writer some very 'novel' formats, and new ones are being developed all the time.

A popular arena for creative writers is within a MUD, an imaginary role-playing environment. This is a text-based environment in which you log on as an imaginary character, one that you create for yourself. Once within the virtual community you can join in the activities of the MUD. It may mean talking to other characters, playing games, puzzle-solving, sharing in creating an online adventure. MUDs started as adventure games but have been developed to provide educational resources and to create interactive creative works. There are now MOOs and several other formats. The online writing community at Nottingham University, called trAce, has an active MUD arena.

A number of websites are now offering electronic publications for sale online. The text is converted into downloadable files that can be opened once the purchase price has been paid, usually by credit card. The author receives a royalty payment on sale, often on a monthly account.

The quality of the services offered by these sites varies. Most will accept an author's manuscript (sent as an email attachment) and from that create a product that can be sold. Many seem to have ignored the need to evaluate and edit such work. The quality of the original work is not important; such companies are looking for volume. It is a new form of vanity publishing.

Whatever the initial teething problems, such facilities offer many writers great opportunities, especially unpublished writers. Their work can be displayed before an audience, where it is hoped that the reader will evaluate it and decide to purchase. Already there are success stories, with many thousands of electronic books being sold online.

These sites offer a replacement publication service. Most do not require an initial investment, others ask for a nominal sum that is much less than that demanded by those sharks of the conventional publishing world: vanity or subsidy publishers. The publisher and author share the risk of failure and take a share in any profits. In a world where it is practically impossible for a new author of creative works to find a publisher they offer a lifeline. How strong it will become is still not clear.

A writer can offer to sell their work on their own website. Although e-commerce (electronic commerce) assumes that payments will be made by credit card this need not be the case. You can always suggest that a cheque or International Money Order is posted to an address, and a disk or an email containing the work will then be sent. Using the web as a brochure, and providing services similar to a mail order company is feasible. Ensure that your ISP allows commercial use of the website.

The internet offers many opportunities to writers. This chapter has looked at the opportunities offered by the internet from the viewpoint of publishing a traditional novel. While that is possible it does not recognise the real potential of this new medium. But it is a good place to start from, providing a firm foothold as the writer steps out into virtual space.

12

CONVENTIONAL PUBLISHING –
HOW WILL IT BE CHANGED?

It is time to say more about conventional publishing and to relate it to our discussion of the internet.

Audience

A writer needs an audience. Who that audience will be and how they will be reached are important questions for every writer to consider. Writing can be a selfish process but the reader is very important and must be considered at all times.

There are nearly 100,000 books published in the UK every year. The number is steadily rising, despite reports that fewer people are reading books. Powers of concentration are said to be waning and every product, including books, seeks to have instant appeal. There would appear to be plenty of opportunity for new writers.

New fiction

Unfortunately very few of the new works of fiction published commercially each year are by new writers. That does not seem to deter the 250,000 hopefuls in the UK who are now writing a novel. Such writers seem oblivious to the fact that they are very unlikely to find a publisher. 'It will be different in my case.' Such optimism is shared within hundreds of writers' circles all over the country and helps to maintain a buoyant magazine industry busily arranging competitions and full of suggestions for budding authors.

There is little financial support available to new writers. The Arts Councils lean towards published authors, often those with work of little commercial appeal. That approach does little to encourage new writing talent but does much to maintain commercial failure. That said, literature receives a poor allocation of cash from such sources compared with other art forms.

Assuming that you have not won the National Lottery, the accepted procedure is that a publisher must be found once 'The Great Work' is completed. Often writers do not seem to care too much about presentation. You must make it easy for the publisher's reader by double-spacing the text, providing wide margins, making sure that the author's name and the title of the book and the page number appears on every page. This is often ignored. The work is usually word-processed so it is readable but the spell-checker was clearly not working and grammar is for kids. Writing is both an art and a craft and it takes time and practice to perfect skills. How many of these writers would join a golf club, buy a set of clubs and expect to be playing in the US Masters golf tournament next year? Yet writers seem to believe that they can perform such miracles in their chosen field.

The covering letter enclosed within the wad of MSS is sometimes as brief as saying, 'Here is my novel for you to publish.' It is no wonder that publishers are tardy in replying to such demands. An explanatory letter sent to a suitable publisher – one that actually publishes novels – together with a synopsis and a sample chapter may have met with a better response.

Publishing today

Publishers' offices are often crammed with unsolicited manuscripts. Many of these are totally unsuitable, and would never be published by that company anyway. The publishing world has changed considerably over recent years. The philanthropic publisher has largely disappeared. Imprints with select lists personally nurtured by a benevolent proprietor are very hard to find. Most have been subsumed within commercial corporations whose primary motivation is to increase turnover and profit. Growth is paramount and product is merely the vehicle used to build the size of the figure on the bottom line.

Within such a company the individual book is of little importance to the company. Once selected for publication it enters into the system. The manuscript is sent to proofreaders, editors and graphic designers who are all likely to be working as freelance agents. Once processed it goes to the printer, then to the distributor and finally on to the shelves of a bookshop. Initially it is likely to appear in just a few selected shops, where it will sit in designated locations waiting for customers to appear. The shop knows how many books each week it will sell from that particular shelf. If the new writer's book has got this far it may have two weeks to prove itself. After that sales will be analysed and if they do not match expectations the remaining copies will be sent away to be pulped. That is the end of the story for that book, and often for that author, heralded with loud cries of 'Next!' from the stockroom.

Who will read?

Although this may sound depressing it is close to the reality that all writers must learn to accept. It returns us to the original question: who will read the work? Once the likely readership is known, the decisions about the publishing method to adopt can be examined. So far this chapter has talked only of creative works. Writers' circles, magazines and university courses are all fixed upon the needs of the creative writer. Yet works of fiction form a very small proportion of the total number of books published. Indeed, full-length novels by new authors are insignificant in number when compared with the total number of books published every year.

The majority of self-published books are autobiographies. These author-publishers have satisfied an inner need to leave a personal record or to record some moment of history in which they were involved. They have also recognised that a commercial publisher is unlikely to be interested in such stories. Self-publishing provides an answer. Increasingly the internet adds value to such enterprises. A self-published wartime memory of time spent in a prisoner-of-war camp in Germany brought together two old comrades. One, now living in Western Australia, had surfed the web and found the biography of his old friend. That reunion was enough to justify the cost of self-publishing the book.

Self-publishers are often experts in their field. The audience they address may be very small, a market not large enough to be commercially viable. Sometimes their views may not be accepted by other scholars. A. D. Walker-Wraight has produced a long list of books about Christopher Marlowe, the Tudor poet and playwright. She suggests that Marlowe was the true author of the works of William Shakespeare. Erudite and well reasoned though her arguments may be, the establishment rejected her thesis. Publishing the work herself allowed her work to be discussed more widely. Now that she can advertise those books on the internet, more and more people can begin to know about, and to understand, her conviction that Marlowe was Shakespeare's author.

Publish yourself

Initially writers should concentrate upon the market for their work that is closest at hand, and that likely to be the most tolerant. Start by publishing for family and friends, moving the circle further outwards if there is a demand.

At its simplest that means printing out A4 word-processed pages, folding them in half and stapling them between 160 gsm card covers.

One booklet, easily produced, to distribute amongst friends. More copies can be photocopied and stapled together in the same way.

Photocopying onwards

Some major photocopier companies such as **Kodak**™ and **Rank Xerox**™ have extended the process to create a book production machine. Kodak's Docutech system will accept word-processed page layouts from a disk. It rapidly photocopies these pages, using paper that will not ripple under the heat of the photocopier engine. Once collated into the final book the pages are bound together. The process glues the edges of the folded pages. With modern adhesives the bound book has a good shelf-life, as the adhesives do not fail after a few months, causing the pages to split apart. Finally the pages are guillotined to form sharp sides to the book, and the paper sheets are glued into the cover. One book is produced. The whole process is very fast.

This is not a perfect process. The computer programming and engineering processes needed to produce these machines are complex. Therefore the machines are both expensive and have a history of failures. However, they offer a cheap and fast means of producing books and booklets. Especially for the sort of material that is likely to change fairly rapidly, so that new editions will be needed at regular intervals. In such cases the fact that the process relies upon graphite powder adhering to paper – and so may ultimately fail – is unimportant.

Digital printing

There are other new processes. Colour photocopiers now add a new dimension, allowing illustrations to be added, and can even be used to produce book covers. Digital printers take information from a computer file and transfer it into a book in a matter of minutes. Such processes will have profound effects upon the publishing industry. Why bother to print several thousand copies of a book at one time? The economies of scale provided by long runs, on offset litho printing machines, are significant. But if the costs of writing, book design, printing, storage and distribution are taken into account the digital printer becomes viable. As the existing digital printing machines are improved upon the gap between conventional and digital printing methods will lessen.

There is also the inertia of convention to overcome. We have always thought of books being produced in long runs and stored on the shelves of warehouses and shops until required. That is the way a book behaves. It sits on a shelf and waits until it is required. This will change as new printing methods become established. And the internet will provide further incentives.

Printing on demand

A new concept is **Printing on demand (POD)** which means that the book is prepared up to the stage when it is ready for printing. It has been written, properly corrected and edited and page designs have been prepared. The next stage is to *print* the book. But that will not take place until an order to purchase a copy is actually received. When that happens the book will be printed and sent to the paying customer. Such a system offers considerable advantages. There is no huge investment in the physical materials used in book production, as the only risk is that of the cost of preparing the book for production. Using digital processing and the internet, that concept can be taken even further. The book is ready to print. There is an advertising campaign, using the conventional methods of book promotion: fliers, advance information sheets, adverts in trade magazines, mailing to libraries and others who may be interested in buying, book launches and authors signing copies during special events. It is also promoted on the internet; with emailings to a range of contacts, including literary editors and librarians, it can be submitted to search engines, with press release material being posted to newsgroups and to sites specialising in such promotions. But no customers copies' are printed until an order is received.

Flexibility of approach

That is still a conventional approach. A major difference could be the way in which the book is published. Years ago we became used to buying audio-cassettes of music, then we slowly moved towards CDs and now new digital systems are appearing. Books will undergo similar changes. A publisher – and this could be the author – might choose to produce the book in the conventional fashion. With several thousand copies of the book stored in the spare bedroom the promotion campaign can get under way. But the book can be left at the pre-print stage and printed only when an order is received. It may make more sense to print, say, 100 copies at a time.

The process can be extended even further. Why bother to print the book at all? It can be prepared for printing and then sold to the final purchasers, who can then be left to print the book themselves. With **Adobe™ Acrobat** the page layout can be retained, and the book can be printed as originally intended. This may seem an onerous option to give the purchaser but a small book of poetry or a list of names and addresses may be more practical, produced this way.

Moving even further away from convention the book can be published as an electronic text; either to be read on a dedicated reader such as those sold by **Softbook** or available to be sold as a downloadable file such as the **1stBooks.com** offer.

Beyond the book

Why stop at such processes? In each case the assumption is that the book will eventually look very much like a conventional book. It may be on screen, or unbound. Every copy may be slightly different, altered to meet the needs of the customer. But it will still look like a book. There are still other ways that can be used.

Audio-cassette books, usually read by professional actors, have seen considerable growth in recent years. Writers can easily produce their own spoken texts, recording them on to a master cassette, which can then be replicated at will. Employing an actor and using a recording studio will greatly improve the final product but the costs are not beyond the cost of a conventional book.

Or you could produce a CD-ROM, allowing audio, graphics, video and text – making a multimedia presentation of the book. Although expensive authoring programs will produce excellent products – provided the operator is competent – using a presentation package such as **Microsoft™ PowerPoint** can also produce a good result.

This may seem overly ambitious but it is not beyond the capabilities of many writers. Those writers who have absorbed the culture of the internet may find this is a logical next step. Until the internet allows fast, cheap transmission of data, CD-ROMs and DVDs offer huge potential. With large storage capacities and fast access times, these disks can allow a writer to provide a multimedia presentation.

Only produce when required

Printing on demand is possible using digital display. The computer is at the heart of the process. It allows the writer to display and sell work online. It can delay printing until an order for the work is actually received, thus reducing initial production costs and allowing the author of the work to experiment with little risk.

This does not remove the need for writers to use publishers. Self-publishing requires special skills and few such books reach their full potential; the tasks of preparing material, marketing and distribution all require special skills. But changes in the relationship between author and publisher may come about as both bring particular skills to the relationship. And publishers are unlikely to disappear.

Just a few copies

Writers should consider producing only a few copies of their work. Short-run printing allows 100 copies of an average novel to be produced for no more than the cost of a holiday, or a set of golf clubs or the membership of a club. Writing is a pleasure and should be regarded as a hobby, not as a potential source of income. Many books can now be produced without using the special skills of a publisher. For most writers 100 copies of their first work will meet all their needs. For the more ambitious a finished book looks so much better than a dog-eared manuscript and can be used as a promotional device alongside the synopsis of their next work. Perhaps writers should regard their early work as disposable indicators of their potential.

13

THE FUTURE

'The web reminds me of early days of the PC industry. No one really knows anything at all. All experts have been wrong.'
Steve Jobs, *Wired*, February 1996.

The internet has changed the face of communication forever. It can certainly be ranked with the invention of the printing press, the telephone and television, for its overall effect on mass media. We know what is possible at the moment, but it is hard to predict where these possibilities will take us in the future. Computers are still the main way that people access the internet, but there are many other internet-enabled devices now available – pagers and cell phones can now send and receive email and access the web. It is possible that the effects of the internet will soon be felt everywhere in your house. ScreenFridge, developed by Electrolux, is effectively an internet icebox that manages your larder. It can email a shopping list to your cyber-supermarket and even negotiate a convenient delivery time that fits in with your daily timetable. To give you a taster of the impact that the internet will have on other areas of your personal life, here are a few numbers to mull over:

- There are 151 million people online, leaping to a projected 230 million by 2001.

- The total revenue in dollars, mainly due to US domination, is somewhere in the region of $7 billion.

- Online banking services are used by 8 million households, rising to 22 million by 2001.

Predictions for the future

If you find those statistics mind-blowing then make a cup of coffee, sit down in a comfortable chair, and run your eyes over a few more:

- There will be an explosion of online commerce, commercial publishing, database distribution, video-conferencing and 3-D environments. Some of these applications are already in use, or are currently under development.

- Many companies are developing secure internet payment systems and the emergence of ecash – the digital equivalent of cash – is more than a distinct possibility. Ecash in your internet bank account will be stored on the hard drive of your computer. When you want to make a payment on the internet, you use ecash. This system will allow you to shop direct from your computer.

- The internet, telephone and television will be linked. In fact some televisions already come with email facilities.

- Intranet/Extranet – there will be 133 million users by 2001. Extranets are web-based systems like intranets but can link up multiple businesses and customers in private, secure areas.

- And strangely enough in the middle of all this growth there is expected to be a 'fall-off' period, when people become sick and tired of the internet and the ongoing band-width problems.

- Online shopping will replace large discount stores. Internet users will make even more purchases over the internet. Seventy per cent of users now shop regularly on the internet.

- Y2K – 15 million nerds are expected to log on simultaneously just to see what's gone wrong.

- As numbers of internet users grow over the coming years a two-tiered web system will develop. One tier, with mid to slow modems of 56K or less, will begin to be left behind, finding more sites that do not perform. The second tier, with high-speed modems, will expect and get more.

But predictions are only predictions and human nature is a funny thing. Any predictions about the internet may be suspect; but the future dictates that whatever the ride, bumpy or smooth, you'd better get a ticket.

Future generations

In 1996, the Philips Company released its vision of the future in the form of a poster showing 48 different kinds of information appliances that would be possible in the future. They classified these appliances into four general categories: personal, domestic, public and mobile. This list included T-shirts embedded with radios or audio chips; smart bathroom mirrors and appliances to monitor weight and blood pressure; postcards that captured sound and image instantly; earplugs that function as in-ear pagers, relaying messages; hot badges loaded with personal information to exchange with other people; emotion containers that would replace photo albums by storing video memories; videophone watches and display glasses which enhance normal sight with a projected layer of information. Amazingly a lot of these technologies have already been realised; some of them – such as a ballpoint pen that records your voice – are already in production.

The internet in the UK

The UK is catching up, slowly but surely, as evidenced by the following statistics:

- Over 6 million adults in the UK have used the internet in the 12 months to June 1997 with the around 9+ million adults expected to have used it by 1999.
  Source: NOP Research

- British use is growing by at least 10–15% a month, the highest sustained growth rate in Europe.
  Source: NOP Research

- The number of households in Britain with access to the internet has more than doubled, from just under 400,000 to 900,000 in 1997.
  Source: NOP Research

- 10 million consumers have made purchases through the internet.
  Source: CommerceNet/Nielsen Media Research

- 25% of all homes in Western Europe will have a connection to the internet by 2001.
  Source: Datamonitor

- 29.6% of users are in education-related occupations.
  27.8% are in a computer-related occupation.
  18.9% are professional.
  10.7% are in management.
  Source: IDC

- 'The popularity of the internet in Europe will increase as quickly as TV did in the '60s.'
  Christian Buerger, Senior Analyst at Datamonitor

- Modem sales are expected to double in the next 12 months.
  Source: Simba Romtec

- The cost of fast modems is dropping by more than 50% each year.

- Commercial internet services are available at local telephone rates in all major towns and cities.

- There are over 90 cybercafés, pubs, restaurants and bookshops in the UK – the highest density of such establishments in the world.

- Every UK school now has an internet connection. Internet access is now as fundamental to school children as a visit to the library.

1999 – What happened and what is likely to happen

- Companies on the internet will continue to consolidate. 1998 was marked by a number of high profile mergers both offline and online. The most noteworthy online merger was undoubtedly that of AOL and Netscape.

- Europe will experience a boom in e-commerce but will continue to lag behind the US.

- Politics will go online and online voting will unroll. The internet will change the face of politics in Europe and the US. As politicians come online they will be forced to interact more with their voters. In Europe, Gallup found that 60 per cent of British adults would like to vote online, and 41 per cent said they would like to interact with their local representative.

● Companies will re-evaluate global policies and small business will surge online. Many smaller companies will find that it is not always to their advantage to have a global presence. Concentrating on local markets and targeting niche communities will become a necessity for small- to medium-size businesses.

● 'Vertical' portals will replace portals and company intranets. While portal mania dominated much of 1998, vertical portals – elaborate company intranets providing syndicated services – will dominate 1999.

● A shift in the profile of internet users will prompt new marketing techniques. The internet will finally reach critical mass in Europe and the US. The profile of the average 'netizen' will change from the slightly atavistic geek to the 'Mom and Pop' user. Women will outnumber men online and this will be reflected in the type of services offered.

● Consumers will retain power as standards escalate. The Christmas holiday in 1998 created such a high level of demand that online suppliers realised they would have to set new standards of service to keep customers happy.

● The internet will mature as a business forum. The early 1998 rocketing of internet stocks is likely to level out and the internet will mature as a forum for conducting business.

● Band-width will dominate the technology market. Higher access speeds and greater band-width have been promised but will be confined to specific areas within the US. Companies with a global reach will continue to maintain fast downloading websites.

● The internet will become the primary source of information. As PCs sell for under $800 and fixed access rates become more widespread, the internet will replace the TV as the primary source of information in the household.

(Information courtesy of NUA internet surveys)

The future of the future

NGI – Next Generation Internet and I2 – Internet2

Over 140 universities in the States teamed up with the US Government and certain members of industry to develop Internet2. This went online in February 1999. It is currently working to enable applications, such as tele-medicine, digital libraries and virtual laboratories that are not possible within today's internet technology. Internet 2 has vast broad-band capabilities that can carry huge amounts of data at speeds many times faster than current modem speeds. It will probably be available for commercial use in a few years. However, Internet2 will not replace the internet; it aims rather to bring together institutions and resources to develop new technologies that can be used with and alongside the global internet. By combining the resources of top universities, industry and government, the US has created a system that will have far-reaching implications for the future of the internet as we know it. The US also hopes to sustain its leadership in internet-working technology at the same time. However, most computer users will no doubt benefit in the long term from any or all of these developments.

Internet2 will no doubt impact on us in many ways in the future.

- Congestion will be reduced because of a much faster replication of information.

- There will be greater security and reliability in email and e-commerce.

- 'Multicast' technology will enable data to be sent to multiple recipients at the same time. (No more low resolution audio and video.)

- 'Tele-immersion': where you enter a fully three-dimensional virtual world and appear to interact with other net users in real time, will replace chat and video-conferencing.

- Within three years researchers will be working on even more powerful systems.

If you want to take a closer look at the future, surf into these sites:
NGI Initiative Home Page
http://ngi.gov

University Corporation for Advanced Internet Development
http://www.internet2.edu/
Internet Society http://www.isoc.org

What does the future hold for the writer?

The future looks good for writers and the internet has opened up a whole new world for them. It has enabled them to communicate with other writers from around the world; it has effectively broken the iron grip that the print-based publishing industry had on the written word. This monopoly restricted the writer to the extent that, if they failed to crack the industry, their only other alternatives lay in self-publishing or seeking out a vanity publisher. Neither of these can be seen as satisfactory.

The internet has provided the writer with a plethora of new markets to consider. All those commercial and business websites need writers to write for them. One only has to look at the content of some of the sites on the internet to realise that although the graphics may be 'out of this world', the written content often leaves a lot to be desired. Graphics are simply not enough to keep a user interested, the content has to be well written and this is where writers should come to the fore.

There are certain elements of the internet that change daily and this is not necessarily an unhealthy factor. The internet's transient character is a process of evolution. Change can be a dynamic element and the internet is largely a force for good. It means that information does not become stagnant or static and this is especially good as far as publishing on the internet is concerned. But it is not usually change for change's sake; the constant ebb and flow of ideas and material found on the internet is providing the writer with a constantly updated supply of new options to consider on a daily basis.

Unfortunately, some sections of the print-based publishing industry have become large, slothful mediums where new writers find it hard to make their mark. Writers are often restricted in their search for recognition by what are seen as 'market trends' within the traditional writing industry; this means that they are forced to consider writing for a specific market, rather than allowing their talent to develop naturally. There are no restrictions of this nature on the internet. A writer should feel able to stretch his legs and on the internet he can do this; he can break all the rules because there are no rules to break. The internet also offers the writer a much more stable base. For instance, e-publishers will often give their authors a longer 'shelf life' than mainstream publishers allow to their authors; there aren't the usual restrictions on articles being reprinted, and self-publishing does not come with the same stigma as it does in the mainstream. For these reasons alone a writer should seriously consider adding the internet to his or her repertoire.

Some future web issues to consider

A Pulitzer Prize for the 'new media'

The Pulitzer Prize committee has debated in the past whether it will accept any new media in future years. As a writer, do you care? The writing, film, TV and journalism industry have their own prizes and it seems to make sense that this new medium should develop its own awards for excellence. This will no doubt happen in future years. The internet needs to be judged by different criteria, such as interactivity, design and writing for the new medium. It would seem to make sense that this new medium is judged by its own people. The film community does not judge the writing community, or vice versa, and so it should be that the new medium is judged by people in that field.

Netizens

Some regard 'netizens' simply as internet users; they can also be referred to as 'digerati' or 'anti-spammers'. However, to qualify one has to become a dedicated internet user, a user who wishes to have a say on internet issues such as copyright, freedom of speech, and spamming, rather than just a person who uses the internet for their own personal use. Netizens defend the internet's right to freedom of speech; they prevent spamming and hacking; they have seen the future and are involved in heavy-duty discussions about its implications. They are in some ways the future politicians of their world. They act to improve the internet and to seek to explain the internet to those who don't understand it. So it is possible for the writer to take this wider view of the internet if they wish to do so. They can become involved in shaping the internet and perhaps seek to establish themselves as 'netizens' by voicing their opinions in the wider forum.

Freedom of speech

Anyone who has access to the internet can have a website. And they have the freedom to publish material of their choice on that site. There are no real restrictions on content. The internet allows anyone who has access to it to use the facilities it provides in pretty much any way they want. You can post a message, send emails, gather information, submit articles, publish your work, and say what you want when you want. It has allowed dissidents a voice, victims a forum, and it provides open discussion of any current affairs issue you choose to mention. It has – in a real, new sense – given the people a voice.

But this has been achieved because an individual can be nameless and faceless on the internet. No one has to know who or what you are; it is possible to preserve your identity or even to lie about your identity and no one will be any the wiser. Unfortunately, this has led to most newsgroups, and USENET in general, becoming almost inoperable. Many groups have been flooded with unrelated posts, crossposting to hundreds of groups, and unscrupulous advertisers' spamming. New users often find themselves causing chaos because they don't know – or don't follow – newsgroup etiquette and are then bombarded with criticism. People begin arguments that take over the group, and these result in bitter and seemingly endless feuding that restricts the free flow of conversation from other users.

The resolution of this problem lies in moderation. The best newsgroups are now moderated; which means that someone, somewhere controls the content and does not allow vicious or childish remarks or arguments to invade the discussion. This means that some freedom of speech will die, but for all those who are on the internet for proper discussion and freedom of ideas, moderation is the key to success. Internet users will probably have to resign themselves to the fact that the future will bring with it new restrictions on their freedom of speech. For some this will mean that the true nature of the internet will be lost; for others it will mean a more regulated and stable community.

Scary stuff

Apparently there are about 30,000 hacker-oriented sites on the internet, and you don't have to be a computer genius to have a go. Some scary facts to consider:

● During the Gulf War, Dutch hackers stole information about US troop movements from the US Defense Department computers and tried to sell it to the Iraqis. The Iraqis thought it was a hoax and turned it down.

● In March 1997, a 15-year-old Croatian youth penetrated computers at a US Air Force base in Guam.

- In 1997 and 1998, an Israeli youth calling himself 'The Analyzer' allegedly hacked into Pentagon computers with help from California teenagers. Ehud Tenebaum, 20, was charged in Jerusalem in February 1999 with conspiracy and harming computer systems.

- In February 1999, unidentified hackers seized control of a British military communication satellite and demanded money in return for control of the satellite. The report was vehemently denied by the British military, which said all satellites were 'where they should be and doing what they should be doing'.

The last word

As the physical world begins to interrelate with the virtual, society will be restructured. Electronic commerce means the demise of the middleman; we will be able to buy direct from the manufacturer wherever we live. Who really needs the services of a bank when electronic cash can be transferred between parties at will? Why build offices or shops? Will our town centres once more become places of social interchange with bars, restaurants and coffee houses replacing the denizens of retail commerce?

Such questions are for all of us. Writers will play their own part in the revolution. The internet offers huge challenges and all writers will need to become involved. Send us an email!**applet** Small software applications that allow data to be manipulated locally on the user's computer, decreasing the band-width needed to run networked programs.

GLOSSARY OF TERMS

attach(ment) An attachment facility allows you to 'attach' one or several files (usually indicated by a paperclip) to your email.

authoring The process of creating a title for distribution.

banner adverts The internet's version of a billboard, usually found on the top of a search engine or a website. It is usually a rectangular box at the top of the page through which to click to another site.

bitmap A way of representing images for the computer. It is essentially the pattern of dots that make up a picture and can be manipulated by a computer.

bookmark A way to list a favourite website that is retained in the browser's bookmark menu for retrieval at a later date.

browser A computer programme use to navigate the WWW and display its content.

chatroom 'rooms' where you can meet and talk online. Post comments onto the screen for other to read.

CD-ROM Any compact disk with data on it. The term CD-ROM usually means a non-audio disk. These days CD-ROM is used in reference to disks containing data that can be used in a computer system.

CD-ROM drive A device that reads data from CD-ROM disks into a computer.

compact disk A plastic disk with a reflective surface on one side that can be encoded and read with a laser beam.

compression A technique for reducing the amount of data needed to store digital information.

cursor A movable pointer symbol on the computer screen used to locate the current screen position of the user. Can indicate a choice or access a hyperlink.

domain name A particular name chosen by you for your website, www.author.co.uk is a domain name. Normally a fee is paid annually for a domain name.

database A library of related information, which can accessed electronically through a computer.

digital In a form capable of being processed by a computer. Data converted to ones and zeros – the only type of information a computer is capable of processing.

drag and drop The process of selecting an object either text or graphic, moving it to another location on the screen, and then releasing it onto another object for any type of processing or re-grouping.

drop-down field An input field in which a pre-existing list of possible selections drops down when the user points to it with the cursor. The user then selects an item from the list.

ebook Any form of electronic book in which contents are stored and played back digitally.

e-cash An electronic form of money – stored on your computer's hard drive.

e-commerce Business conducted solely on the internet

encoding Converting information to a digital format capable of being used by a particular system.

e-publisher A publisher who publishes work on the internet to be downloaded from their web-site by interested parties. They do not publish work in print form.

e-zine An electronic magazine using much the same format as print based magazines delivered via email.

FAQ Frequently Asked Questions – a file containing background information on a topic.

floppy disk A magnetic disk that can store date and can be removed and transported to another computer that uses the same operating system.

freespace Space made available, either by an ISP or a search engine, to people who use their email facilities enabling them to create a website for no cost.

guidelines A series of requirements to follow when submitting work to a website or an ezine – each publication or site will have their own guidelines.

FTP File Transfer Protocol - an original internet protocol used to transfer date files in an non-interactive fashion.

hardware All of the components of the physical computer of machine, such as the processor, the memory chips, and the monitor.

home page The first and main document that appears on a website, often directing the user to other pages.

host A main computer used to control communications.

hot spot A place on the screen (word, phase, graphic) that contains a hyperlink. The hot spot can be linked to text elsewhere or it can trigger playback of an audio or video clip.

HTML Hypertext Markup Language – the language used to code text files, primarily used for documents found on the web.

HTTP HyperText Transfer Protocol – An international standard transmission protocol used for web files.

hyperlink A link between two related points in a database. The user can point with a cursor to one link and by pressing a button while the cursor is positioned over the first link, access the second link.

hypermedia Multimedia that is interconnected by hyperlinks.

hypertext Text that uses links to connect to other, often elaborating text.

interactive Media that responds to the user. Interactive media are connected via a system of links. They respond when the user points a cursor and clicks on them.

interactive fiction Fiction that is created online.

internet A series of interconnected networks with local, regional and national networks, using the same telecommunications protocol (TCP/IP). Provides email, remote login and file transfer. The web is communicated via the internet.

internet2 Internet2 will enable applications, such as tele-medicine, digital libraries and virtual laboratories that are not possible within today's internet technology. It will not replace the internet as we know but rather enhance its original capabilities.

internet Address A unique numeric address that identifies a computer connected to the internet.

Intranet A Computer network that is used for internal internet communication.

Java A programming language developed and promoted by Sun Microsystems for sending programs called 'applets' over the internet. These applets are sent in partially compiled form and are then fully compiled by the user's computer.

keywords A list of all the words and short phrases that can be chosen to describe your site. It tries to match the words inserted into search engine query boxes

link A hypertext path connecting one part of a document to other documents.

mailing list Sends an individual copy of a message to a subscriber usually arriving as an email.

manuscript format In what form a particular e-zine or web-site wishes to receive manuscripts. Double spaced, etc.

menu A text or graphic screen that lists choices for users, which can be selected by pointing with the cursor and clicking.

moderate A system used to control the content of postings on newsgroups, or used to 'police' a chat room. These moderated groups are usually controlled by the presence of a 'moderator' who makes sure everyone behaves themselves.

multimedia A medium which combines text, audio and video in an interactive product or service.

netizen A term used on the internet to describe dedicated users.

new media Any electronic media employing interactive means for its expression.

news groups A world wide distributed bulletin board system allowing internet users around the world to submit messages to certain newsgroups; these messages are delivered to every internet hosts that wants them.

online A service which provides access to a database over telephone lines such as when connecting to the internet.

page counter A page counters measure how many people visit a website.

portal sites Provide an opening page to a web browser that can be tailored to individual needs.

posting Putting a message on a newsgroup or submitting details about yourself to a ezine or job market.

Printing on demand (POD) A book is prepared up to the stage when it is ready for printing. Printing will not take place until an order to purchase a copy is actually received.

search engine The computer program that allows the location and retrieval of information in a database, such as Yahoo UK.

server A computer connected to a network and used to provide services such as a web page or directing email.

spamming A technique used by many companies to advertise their products via email, usually done anonymously and in large numbers.

submission guidelines a list of requirements needed when submitting a manuscript to a particular online magazine, ezine or website.

tree-fiction A type of online interactive novel developed on the internet. Allows the reader to control how the story will develop.

tag Any of many code strings embedded in an HTML document which determine graphical layout, hyperlinks, and embedded objects such as Java written applets or multimedia file downloading and opening.

TCP/IP A set of protocol that standardise data transfer between computers connected to the internet

title An electronic work, for either CD-ROM or online distribution, that employs new media

URL Uniform Resource Locator – an address describing a specific document on the Web.

USENET A large number of globally available newsgroups in which users may post and read messages.

user The person who navigates the web or uses a software program.

VDU Visual display unit – the screen.

web browser A software program used to access the web and use hyperlinks to more from site to site. Also used in conjunction with software plug-in programs to listen to audio files, view video programs.

web server A computer holding web pages and used to distribute them over a network.

website A collection of inter-linked files and documents written with HTML and available on the internet.

Windows A user-friendly operating system used in most computers with Intel-made CPU's.

World Wide Web WWW – The world-wide network of computers and documents that uses HTML markup language.

INDEX